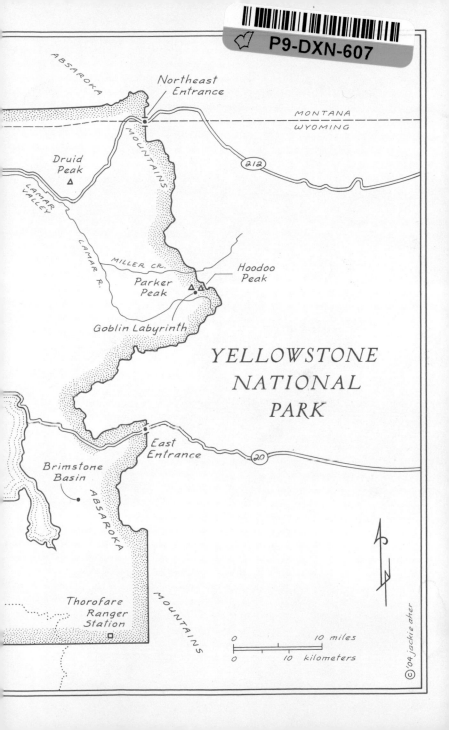

ABSAROKA

Northeast
Entrance

MONTANA
WYOMING

212

Druid
Peak △

LAMAR VALLEY

MOUNTAINS

LAMAR R.

MILLER CR.

Parker
Peak △ △

Hoodoo
Peak

Goblin Labyrinth

YELLOWSTONE
NATIONAL
PARK

East
Entrance

20

Brimstone
Basin

ABSAROKA

Thorofare
Ranger
Station

MOUNTAINS

0   10 miles
0   10 kilometers

© '04 jackie aher

Lost in My Own Backyard

Lost in My Own Backyard

A WALK IN YELLOWSTONE NATIONAL PARK

Tim Cahill

CROWN JOURNEYS

CROWN PUBLISHERS · NEW YORK

Published by Crown Journeys, an imprint of Crown Publishers,
New York, New York.
Member of the Crown Publishing Group, a division of Random House, Inc.
www.crownpublishing.com

CROWN JOURNEYS and the Crown Journeys colophon are registered
trademarks of Random House, Inc.

Portions of "Backcountry Trails" have appeared in slightly different form in
National Geographic Adventure magazine.

Printed in the United States of America

Design by Lauren Dong

Map by Jackie Aher

Library of Congress Cataloging-in-Publication Data
Cahill, Tim.
    Lost in my own backyard : a walk in Yellowstone National Park / Tim
Cahill.—1st ed.
1. Yellowstone National Park—Description and travel. 2 Yellowstone
National Park—History. 3. Natural history—Yellowstone National Park.
4. Cahill, Tim—Travel—Yellowstone National Park. 5. Walking—
Yellowstone National Park. 6. Hiking—Yellowstone National Park.
7. Camping—Yellowstone National Park. I. Title. II. Crown Journeys series
F722.C15   2004
978.7'52—dc22   2003025779

ISBN 1-4000-4622-X

10   9   8   7   6   5   4   3   2

First Edition

To my father,
Richard J. Cahill

CONTENTS

Contents

Lost in My Own Backyard

Introduction

YELLOWSTONE NATIONAL PARK AND VICINITY IS THE
largest intact temperate-zone ecosystem in the northern hemisphere. It is a vast area of earthly riches
almost beyond imagining, a natural playground complete with geysers and thermal features so strange that
early white visitors referred to the area as "Wonderland." There are herds of bison and elk, there are
beaver and wolves and marmot and osprey and eagles:
there is the whole complement of North American
fauna. It is not an amusement park, however, and it's a
good idea to pay attention. Yellowstone is a place
where the unwary or unlucky can get mauled by a
bear, gored by a bison, stomped by a moose, or bitten
by a rattlesnake. People also fall off cliffs, freeze to
death, and die in avalanches. *Death in Yellowstone,* a
book by Lee Whittlesey, chronicles all manner of
mishap, but it seems that the easiest way to die in the

park is to fall into the water some distance from shore. The temperature of Yellowstone Lake, for instance, averages about 41 degrees. You don't last long in that kind of water.

I bring this up at the beginning because it is important. Part of the joy of walking in Yellowstone is that it is still, for the most part, a wilderness, which means that it is untamed, which in turn means that it is not impossible to get hurt, even if you follow all the rules. Thus the wilderness that is Yellowstone Park affirms our mortality. That is why walking its trails makes us feel so damn alive.

I have not tried to write a guide to the park. Others have done that and done it so well that anything I say would be redundant. I invite you to turn to "A Selected Yellowstone Bookshelf" at the back of this book for a list of great guidebooks. You will want to know about where to camp, how much things cost, what sorts of accommodations are available, and such like. Books in the back present all this information.

I have also listed a number of trail guides. I use every one mentioned because each is a little different from the others and excellent in its own manner. You'll find books on the list about the history of the park and about the biology and the geology of Yellowstone. I hope my own idiosyncratic little book will spur you to explore the park, to enjoy it, and to begin doing your own research into those areas that most enthrall and charm you. The books I've listed are only a start. My friend Tom Murphy has an entire room devoted to books on Yellowstone, to his wife's immense annoyance.

Tom and I both live in a town about 50 miles north of the park and therefore consider Yellowstone to be our backyard. Tom, who is best known for his photography in Yellowstone, is also a guide in the park. When not shepherding clients, he likes to bushwhack off trail and "poke around." I once asked him if he'd ever been lost. "No," he said thoughtfully, "but there were times I didn't know exactly where I was."

That's happened to me as well. I've spent entire afternoons not knowing exactly where I was, which is to say, I was lost in my own backyard. This shouldn't happen if you stay on the major trails. But you may find yourself lost in thought, or in sheer astonishment. And here's the big idea for Americans: Yellowstone was the world's first national park. It was established, by an act of Congress, on March 1, 1872. The park was expressly put aside "for the benefit and enjoyment of the people." That makes Yellowstone Park America's backyard. Your backyard.

So let's go take a walk in the backyard. Let's get lost together.

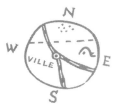

The Trails

Day Hikes

Mount Washburn

A QUARTER CENTURY AGO I MOVED TO A SMALL town just north of Yellowstone Park. I didn't know much about wildlife back then and honestly couldn't tell a mule deer from an antelope. I wasn't certain why Yellowstone contained more geysers than anyplace else on earth. I was unaware that there was a huge lake, one of the largest alpine lakes on earth, up there in the pines. I didn't know much.

But I wasn't a tourist. Oh, no. I was much too cool for that. I never went to Yellowstone specifically to look at, what?—mud pots, or Old Faithful, or various thermal springs. It always seemed to me like that had somehow "been done," and that serious persons, like myself, went into the backcountry, and we did that specifically to avoid all those other persons who didn't know that gaping at geysers or giggling at the flatulent-sounding mud pots was for—well, for tourists, who were somehow inferior.

In fact, the places where tourists customarily go are supremely worth seeing even if you have to share the wonder. That is the conclusion I've come to after a quarter century of puttering around in the park. Oh, I've been out in the backcountry quite a bit, and I've seen the tourist attractions, all of them, several times. I just didn't know how to look at them. I was lost in my own backyard.

I wish someone had just slapped me early on. Well, perhaps I could have done without the slap, but it would have been okay if someone wiser in the ways of the park had just shown me certain things and told me to shut up and listen. *Stop being so damn superior. You're acting like a jerk.*

I have, in fact, a long-standing fantasy in which I take the younger version of myself up to the park and show him the one thing he truly has to understand. It would probably be a hassle getting him through the entrance and up to the summit of Mount Washburn. He'd be asking questions and trying to stop for a walk every time he saw a back-country trailhead. This young guy would be distracted. I'd have to talk with him in a severe manner.

I imagine it would go like this:

Okay, shut up, we're going to the park, and it's going to be a couple of hours of driving, and I'm not going to let you talk about anything at all because you are just going to get all enthralled with this or that and lose the central theme. So here we go, and you might just as well be blindfolded, because we are not going to talk about the mountains that run on either side of Paradise Valley as we rise up Yellowstone River toward the entrance to Yellowstone Park. Oh, those are antelope over there.

Look, stop complaining. I'm taking you twenty-five years closer to figuring out the geological essence of the park. You don't care about geology? How about the end of civilization as we know it? No, I'm not kidding you. The end of civilization as we know it! Sure, right, make fun. Just another damn thing to worry about. Dumb butt.

Here's the north entrance the park. We'll stop, I'll show my National Park Pass to the ranger in the little guardhouse. Yeah, she's attractive, I agree. Some of these lady rangers, I have to admit: I mean, if you've got a thing for women in uniform . . .

Wait. See how easy it is to let things distract you from the central point? Now we're passing the forty-fifth parallel, right at the sign there—halfway between the equator and the north pole—and those are elk emerging out of the steam, which comes from thermal springs dropping into the river, and yes, you can bathe in the hot pots there, where the thermal water drops into the river, but that's not why we've come to the park today. Don't those elk moving through the steam look like they're in some kind of movie about supernatural beings?

But we're getting distracted.

And now here we go: we're driving through the little administrative village of Mammoth. Yes, it's named for those steaming terraces of multicolored rock looming up over there to our right. Mammoth Hot Springs. Sure, we could stop and take a walk, but there are wooden stairs and wooden walkways and you have to stay on the trail and there'll probably be a lot of people all bunched together looking at the delicate colors of the various thermal pools up on top of the terraces and you'll have to hear people say, "Kinda pretty, huh," and so you don't want to go up there, do you? You're too cool for that Disneyland sort of stuff, right?

See, that's what I mean. I was the same way when I was you twenty-five years ago. Exactly the same way. No Old Faithful for me. Been there, done that, now I'm too cool. This, I've come to realize, is a moronic attitude. That's why we're going where we're going today.

What? No, that's a coyote. Wolves are bigger. There're some bison over there. Ignore them, please, as much as you can ignore fifty or sixty animals weighing up to two thousand pounds apiece. Biggest land animal in North America. We'll deal with them later. We're on our way to Tower Junction, then we'll turn south and stop near the top of Dunraven Pass, and then we'll climb to the summit of Mount Washburn. Why? Because our sole ambition this trip is to begin the process of coming to grips with some of the most significant and convulsive cataclysms that ever occurred on the face of the earth.

But see, here's the problem with Yellowstone. You can start off on a trip with every intention of trying to understand the ultimate and end up studying wildflowers. The whole park is an embarrassment of wonders.

Okay, so here we are at Dunraven Pass, 8,895 feet in elevation, and here's where we'll park. Then we'll walk up to the top of Mount Washburn. The guide books say the walk to the fire lookout on the summit rises about 1,400 feet and should take about two hours (much less if you're acclimated), and the view from the summit, at 10,243 feet, is said to be soul-stirring.

Yeah, I know, it isn't exactly your idea of climbing a mountain. This is just a big wide trail, and it used to be a stagecoach road when it was built back in 1905.

See those old clumps of asphalt? In the 1920s, when they let cars into the park, people drove up to the top. They drove up in reverse, because Model T Fords didn't have fuel pumps and you couldn't get gas to the engine on these steep slopes.

There's a sign at the trailhead that says, in effect, that Mount Washburn is a "bear frequenting" area and that it is not impossible to be eaten by a grizzly while walking up this trail. I think such signs make one alert. If you tend to worry about bears, and you should, the first part of the trail may seem a little claustrophobic. It is in deep woods, but it eventually emerges onto grasslands set in long sloping aprons, and for most of the summer and early fall these areas are alive with wildflowers. Some say this is the best place in the park to see these flowers, the colors swirling and intertwining like those on an intricate Persian carpet.

Occasionally we'll get a view of the fire lookout up top, a two-story building with floor-to-ceiling windows, quite a ways off. We've been at it for an hour and a half now and passed several people, except for that disgustingly fit couple who were running. Running uphill, hard. Something seriously wrong with those people. Something wrong with the slow-pokes we passed, too. We're walking at the proper pace, the Cahill pace.

Now we've got about 300 more feet to the summit, and it's a steep 300 feet. The trees here—the

Engelmann spruce, the whitebark pine, and the sub-
alpine fir—are all stunted and twisted, no more than
six feet high, just barely clinging to life on the slope of
the mountain. And now the trees are gone, and on
either side of the trail the land is lumpy with little
hillocks of alpine tundra. Tiny white flowers, smaller
than a dime, are all hunkered down low in the rocks
to avoid the wind and catch the sun.

The fire lookout is glassed in, and it feels good to
stand inside, out of the wind, and look out to the
south. There are a few other folks up here, and some
of them are signing the guestbook. Only a few hundred have signed the book in the past month, though
Mount Washburn is one of the most popular backcountry trails in the park. An estimated ten thousand
people make the climb every year. Folks who sign the
guestbook have come from Japan and Poland and
Switzerland and Connecticut and Oregon and Virginia. There is even some drama in the comments:
"Wow! I wish my husband was here. He locked the
keys in the car . . . so my six year old son and I came
alone while he worked it out. He should have come
with us!" Hey, just kick in the window. This is a once-
in-a-lifetime experience.

Outside, on the rocks under the lookout, are three
or four little furballs, pikas, scrambling frenetically about
on the talus slope. These small rodents have one of
those jet-propelled metabolisms: they do not hibernate.

They just keep busy all winter, burning hot, scampering over the rocks, under the snow. They don't run fast like hares, but they can outmaneuver most predators on rocky slopes.

In the alpine meadow off to the west are half a dozen bighorn sheep. No rams. Only females and juveniles. They are golden brown in color and lying in the grass, which is almost exactly the same shade of gold. You'd miss them if you scanned the field too quickly.

Washburn is named for General Henry Washburn, the surveyor general of the Montana Territory, who led a volunteer group of citizen explorers from Montana into the Yellowstone country in 1870 to investigate rumors of steam erupting out of the ground and other seemingly improbable wonders. The group had heard rumors of a great lake, but they weren't finding it. Washburn climbed the mountain we're standing on and returned to tell everyone that he had seen the lake. Nathaniel Langford, who was along on the trip, later wrote a book about this pioneering expedition and said that Washburn's information, delivered directly from the summit of the mountain, "has quieted our dread apprehensions. . . . We have spontaneously and by unanimous vote given the mountain the name by which it will hereafter be known, 'Mount Washburn.'"

So we've got pika and bighorn sheep, and a trail that rises 1,400 feet from forest through abundant fields of wildflowers and into alpine tundra. There's plenty of history here, too, not to mention a view that a later explorer, General William Strong, described as "Wonderland. Grand, glorious, and magnificent." He also said another true thing: "no pen can write it—no language describe it."

Many visitors know that most of what we now call Yellowstone Park is the caldera of a giant volcano and that all of the park's spouting geysers and colorful hot springs and bubbling mud pots are evidence of volcanism very close to the surface of the earth. We all know that.

If you're like me—and of course you are—you will spend years attempting to visualize the eruption that created the park. You will conjure up in your mind a great big huge gigantic cone-shaped mountain. This mountain would have had foothills to the south, somewhere around Jackson Hole, Wyoming. It would have extended to the north about 50 miles into Montana. This is where my imagination always failed me in the past. The base of the volcano that left a crater nearly the size of Yellowstone, 2.22 million acres, would have had to be several hundred miles in diameter. Mountains aren't several hundred miles in diameter. Mountain ranges are several hundred miles long. But individual mountains that size don't exist and never have. I just couldn't see it, and for a very good reason.

It didn't happen that way.

The way it must have happened, according to some geology texts I've been studying, can best be seen from the top of Mount Washburn, at 10,243 feet. So, okay. Look to the south: there's the bulk of Yellowstone, which is—this is surprising to many people—a rather flat rolling plain. Absaroka Mountains to the east. There's the Grand Canyon of the Yellowstone River down there, and part of Yellowstone Lake, and far to the south the Grand Teton range of mountains. If it is clear enough, you'll see Old Faithful throw a column of boiling water and steam into the air.

The nearest peak to the south is Mount Sheridan, about 37 miles away. It is almost exactly as high as Mount Washburn, give or take about 65 feet. Washburn slopes north, and the southern edge is more abrupt. Sheridan slopes to the south. If you were to clap these two mountains together, you'd have one ordinary roundish mountain.

This fact, among others, has led some geologists to wonder if a whole mountain range had once connected Washburn and Sheridan. And if it had, what in God's name happened to the intervening 37 miles' worth of mountains?

The answer is: they blew up. They blew up, and then they collapsed. It happened very quickly. I'm not talking quickly in geological time: it was very probably a matter of hours. Boom, and then there was ash in the air and ash covering the earth from the Pacific Ocean to the Gulf of Mexico. That was about 640,000 years ago. Geologists know this because they can measure the age of rocks.

The eruption blew off the south side of Washburn, the north side of Sheridan, and everything in between went all to hell. It was one of the biggest eruptions in the history of the earth. But there was no immense cone-shaped mountain.

More than likely it was all the result of an ongoing plumbing problem called the Yellowstone Hotspot. Geologists speculate that the earth's molten core sprang a leak about 25 million years ago. A plume of fiery liquefied rock rose toward the surface of the earth in what is essentially a kind of narrow chimney. About 10 million years ago the molten rock reached the surface of the earth, where it spread out in an immense bowl. The writer Bill Bryson has aptly described the hotspot as looking rather like a martini glass. There are about forty active hotspots on earth at present. They are all located under oceans—except for the one under Yellowstone.

In this hell below the surface, molten rock smoldered close to the crust of the earth, and lighter properties, steam and gases of various sorts, rose to the top of the martini glass. These elements wanted to expand, to explode, but were constrained by the weight of the mountains above. They pushed upward. The land began to rise, humping up like a hissing cat. Ring fractures, great cracks in the earth, formed out at the fringes of the areas where the earth rose.

John Good and Kenneth Pierce describe what happened next in a nicely compact text with an ungainly title, *Interpreting the Landscape: Recent and Ongoing Geology of Grand Teton and Yellowstone National Parks.* Imagine, the authors suggest, a bottle of carbonated water shaken vigorously until the cap blows off. The pressure on the dissolved carbon dioxide (the carbonation) is relieved, and a mass of bubbles and liquid jet up out of the mouth of the bottle. In Yellowstone, when the cap blew, immense fountains of burning hot gases and molten rock and ash blasted into the stratosphere and were carried around the world. (There were likely several years of volcanic winter, when this airborne ash blotted out the sun.) Ash fall covered North America from what is now Saskatchewan to the Gulf of Mexico, from the Pacific Ocean to Iowa.

"Nearer the vents," say Good and Pierce in a memorable description, "fiery clouds of dense ash, fluidized by the expanding gas, boiled over crater rims and rushed across the countryside at speeds of over one hundred miles an hour, vaporizing forests, animals, birds, and streams into varicolored puffs of steam."

Meanwhile, when the underlying pressure was released, what was left of the mountain range between Washburn and Sheridan simply collapsed, slumping into the top of the martini glass. Did the eruption relieve all the pressure? Nope. You can still see evidence of molten activity near the earth's surface in the geyser basins and thermal features of Yellowstone Park. The hotspot is still there. Pressures may still be building.

What this means is that when you walk around in the park today, you are, in effect, standing atop the largest active supervolcano on earth. Is there a chance that it will blow again anytime soon, causing a volcanic winter that would decimate crops worldwide and bring unimaginable famine to the world? An eruption that would bury Nebraska in eight feet of ash, as it did 640,000 years ago? A blast that would turn me and everyone I know living in proximity to the park into "varicolored puffs of steam"? Could that happen?

Oh yeah.

There have actually been three cataclysmic supervolcanic eruptions in Yellowstone and vicinity in the recent geological past. The Huckleberry Ridge eruption may have been the most massive volcanic event in the whole long history of earth. It happened about 2.1 million years ago. The Mesa Falls eruption occurred 1.3 million years ago, and the one I've been describing, the Lava Creek event, happened about 640,000 years ago. Do the math, and you'll see there were 800,000 years between Huckleberry Ridge and Mesa Falls. About 650,000 years between Mesa Falls and Lava Creek. You don't have to be especially handy with numbers to see that these eruptions are getting closer together in time. Some texts are willing to say that there's a cataclysmic supervolcanic eruption in Yellowstone every 600,000 years or so. I don't have to tell you again that the last one was 640,000 years ago.

Which means that we're about due. Just to put everything in context, an eruption of Huckleberry Ridge dimensions would mean the end of civilization as we know it. This is something to think about when you're standing on top of Mount Washburn staring south at 37 miles of mountains that no longer exist.

The thermal features of Yellowstone are unpredictable, unstable, and entirely fascinating. With this in mind, I don't really mind sharing the boardwalk. We're all just potential puffs of steam anyway, and the earth is mighty beyond our imagining.

Norris Geyser Basin

M ORE THAN LIKELY YOU ARE GOING TO DRIVE
to Yellowstone. There are several entrances,
several ways to camp, several places to stay, and advice
about arriving by car is beyond the scope of this book.
For more information on these basics, I strongly recommend the newly released guidebook *Lonely Planet
Yellowstone and Grand Teton National Parks* (see "A
Selected Yellowstone Bookshelf").

Because it is likely that you will drive, I am going
to suggest the road you want, which comprises the
classic tour of the park. It is the drive I use to intro-
duce visiting friends to Yellowstone: it provides a general idea of the area's geography and geology, the
wildlife and the wonder.

The Grand Loop road forms a kind of figure eight
around the park, and was designed in 1886 by Lieutenant
Daniel Kingman. I like to think of it as a brilliantly

conceived exercise in connecting the dots of Wonderland. This 142-mile road passes almost every type of thermal feature, mountain, and wildlife habitat in Yellowstone. It travels past the Norris Geyser Basin (my favorite boardwalk in the park and currently the hottest, or so I imagine, since part of it was closed to tourists in the summer of 2003 due to unpredictable thermal activity). Grab a free brochure, and read the informative signs.

In the early winter of 2002 I was treated to an off-boardwalk tour of an off-limits thermal area near Norris. My guide was Patrick Doss, former Yellowstone Park geologist. Walking on the thin white sand, a silica-based crust called sinter, Doss measured the temperature of various hot pools, while I walked carefully in his steps. It is possible to break through the crust of sinter and—worst-case scenario—fall into boiling water below. Mostly, Doss told me, geologists who concern themselves with thermal features can be distinguished by the various degrees of burns on their lower legs.

If these professionals sometimes miscalculate, visitors—especially first-time visitors—have made fatal errors in the space of a few steps. It really is best to stay on the boardwalk.

Contemplating the geothermal wonders of Norris can occupy the better part of an afternoon or, if you are Patrick Doss, the better part of a lifetime.

It's easy enough to get there, but the Grand Loop can be highly annoying to drive. People who see a moose or an elk or a bear or a bighorn sheep or a herd of bison or a wolf—people who see wildlife—simply slam on the brakes in the middle of the road. For this reason, you want to drive the Grand Loop at a crawl when there is any traffic at all. Anything over 45 miles per hour is both illegal and silly. Creep along. I hesitate to say this in a book devoted to walking, but visitors are likely to see more wildlife from the car than on foot.

Whenever a creature makes an appearance near the road—especially charismatic megafauna, which is to say, things generally hairy and bigger than a human—there will be a traffic jam of hopeless proportions. You might as well pull over and join the orgy of roadside gang photography taking place. Watching my fellow visitors interact with wildlife is often aggravating. No matter how many times people have been warned about the dangers, they tend to take chances. For a picture. Someone carrying a little snapshot camera will approach a herd of two thousand-pound bison, seemingly unaware that the creatures can outrun a horse in a sprint. No matter. The person will move closer, then closer yet, trying to frame the animal in the camera lens. Such people are going to get hurt. I call the lumps they take "Instamatic" injuries.

Bison may seem indolent, even lazy. But then they abruptly decide you need to be gored. People are frequently injured and sometimes killed by bison in Yellowstone. Here's a biologist's hint on watching bison: keep your distance. Watch the ruff around the animal's neck: if it rises, that's a good time to retreat. If the tail goes up, it means "charge" or "discharge."

On the other hand, listening to tourists you will sometimes glean information unavailable in any text. I once heard a father explain to a boy I took to be his son that the moose we were watching was a "mature elk." According to this gentleman, an elk's horns flatten out as he ages. Still, any sort of misinformation is preferable to the terrifying Instamatic situation in which a parent encourages a child to approach a bison or bear or moose so that both the child and the animal are in the same frame.

It happens. I have heard one story, totally unconfirmed, of a father trying to place his young daughter on a bison's back. It is said that the father was injured. I like to think he was beaten savagely by onlookers, but that probably didn't happen. Another story has it that a young man tried to put a necklace of beer can pop-tops around a bison's neck. I was never able to confirm this, either. The Park Service is often circumspect in describing how an injury occurred. But for a look at what can happen if you are dull enough (or simply unlucky), please read Lee Whittlesey's book, *Death in Yellowstone.*

So my drive along the Grand Loop is always an exercise in wonder at the dull and luckless who, I always imagine, are one charge away from a lingering death in a nearby hospital. It's the same feeling I get while watching a horror movie, when the frightened young woman decides she'll hide *in the basement*. No, no, don't do that! There's an ax murderer wearing a hockey mask down there!

Still, I never tell people what to do—would they listen anyway?—and I generally try to get the hell out before anyone gets hurt. It is a great wonder of nature that more people aren't injured in Yellowstone. They're out there trying every day, going down into the figurative basement, where the figurative ax murderer is waiting for them with his figurative ax. Except instead of ax murderers, the dullest of the visitors are dealing with a herd of bison, a nearby grizzly bear, or an enraged moose.

The Upper Geyser Basin
and Old Faithful

S O YOU'LL SEE SOME INTERACTION BETWEEN wildlife and visitors along the Grand Loop, which will eventually sweep you past the entrance to Old Faithful and the Upper Geyser Basin. Roger and Carol Anderson, in *A Ranger's Guide to Yellowstone Day Hikes,* say that "geologically speaking, the Upper Basin is one of the most extraordinary places on earth." It contains over 25 percent of the world's geysers.

The basin is worth looking at through the eyes of Nathaniel Langford, a member of the 1870 Washburn expedition to the park: "We had within a distance of fifty miles seen what we believed to be the greatest wonders of the continent." But they hadn't yet seen Old Faithful. "Judge then," Langford wrote, "our aston-ishment on entering this basin, to see, at no great dis-tance before us, an immense body of sparkling water, projected suddenly and with terrific force into the air." Langford and his colleagues found "a thousand hot springs of various sizes and character."

It was because of these features that the U. S. Congress established the world's first national park in Yellowstone in 1872. This has been called "the best idea America ever had." The quote is attributed to several different persons, as great quotes often are. The congressional act resolved that geysers and geothermal features "in the region of the headwaters of the Yellowstone River" should be "reserved and withdrawn from settlement, occupancy or sale" and "set apart as a public park or pleasuring ground for the benefit and enjoyment of the people."

It is interesting to note that the delegate to Congress from what was then the Montana Territory felt it necessary to draw the bill up in a hurry. We tend to think that it must have been an easy decision to set aside some remote western land that few people even knew about, but, incredibly, even back then commercial pressures were building. The Honorable William H. Claggett, the Montana delegate, later wrote that in the fall of 1870 he knew of two men from the nearby town of Deer Lodge who'd gone into the Firehole Basin, near several of the most spectacular geyser basins, and "cut a large number of poles, intending to come back next summer and fence in the tract of land containing the principal geysers and hold possession for speculative purposes."

There wasn't really any time to lose.

The idea of Yellowstone National Park may have first been proposed in 1865 by acting territorial governor Thomas Meagher. But the most compelling story is one told by Nathaniel Langford. On September 19, 1870, Washburn's exploratory party was camped where the Firehole and Gibbon Rivers join. Some expedition members proposed to take up plots of land at the prominent points of interest, whereupon another member, Cornelius Hedges, said there ought to be no private ownership and that the whole area ought to be set aside as a national park.

Retired park historian Aubrey Haines found no mention of this momentous discussion—the best idea America ever had—in the diaries of any members of the expedition. Cornelius Hedges, for instance, wrote: "Mon. 19 . . . no fish in river. Grub getting very thin."

No, this was simply a good idea whose time had come. Yellowstone was the perfect location. While there were some hot springs in California, some bubbling mud pots in Italy, and a few geyser fields in Iceland and New Zealand, there was nothing on earth like Yellowstone. It contains ten thousand thermal features: more mud pots, fumaroles, and geysers than exist in all the rest of the earth combined. Sixty percent of the world's geysers are concentrated in Yellowstone.

But in the mid- to late 1800s, few educated people believed that such features existed anywhere.

John Colter, who left the Lewis and Clark party (with permission), may have been the first Euro-American to set foot in what is now the park. That was in the winter of 1807–1808. His description of the thermal features was generally scoffed at for many years, and the region was known as "Colter's Hell." This was the form sarcasm took at the time.

In the 1830s the tales of fur trappers and mountain men—Jim Bridger and Osborne Russell—were discounted as hyperbole: the exaggerations of men engaged in the continuing western tradition of deceiving the dude. In 1869 the Folsom, Cook, and Peterson party explored the park. David Folsom and Charles Cook wrote an article from their diaries and submitted it to the *New York Tribune* and *Harper's Magazine*. Both publications, according to Aubrey Haines, refused the article because "they had a reputation they could not risk with such unreliable material." I have always heard that *Harper's* responded, "We do not publish fiction." I have not been able to confirm the quote, but it is still a good story and reflects the general population's lack of faith in the proposition that there are places on earth where hot water erupts out of the ground.

The Washburn party followed the Folsom party's tracks in 1870, and its reports were taken seriously. Dr.

Ferdinand Hayden, director of the U. S. Geological Survey, heard Nathaniel Langford lecture on his travels in Colter's Hell, and was convinced of the man's veracity. In 1871 he successfully petitioned Congress to fund the first scientific expedition into the region. Along on that expedition, which Hayden led, were photographer William Jackson and the celebrated artist Thomas Moran. Hayden's report, Jackson's photographs, and Moran's painting shredded the fabric of doubt. President Ulysses S. Grant signed the landmark Yellowstone Act on March 1, 1872.

I thought I was pretty smart moving to Montana in 1978 and buying a house not far outside the park. I also have a cabin on the edge of the Absaroka-Beartooth Wilderness, which abuts the park. I think it's fair to say, as I have, that Yellowstone is my backyard. I don't claim an exclusive on the backyard situation: I've also pointed out that, if you are an American, Yellowstone is your backyard as well.

I thought of that not long ago while reading *The Wolves of Yellowstone,* a book by Michael Phillips and Douglas Smith. Readers who have not been in a coma for the past twenty years may be familiar with the controversy leading up to the reintroduction of the wolf to the park in 1995.

Michael Phillips had the tough task of talking to local ranchers, the folks who live and grow stock near

the park. Most of them did not support wolf reintroduction, though an enormous majority of Americans
did. "Local folks," Phillips writes, "who have to live
with the wolves" believe they should have the final
say. Not so, Phillips responded. In America everyone
has a vote, "and this right allows ranchers to partici-
pate in decisions on resources throughout the United
States. This," Phillips says dryly, "was of little comfort
to them." The ranchers quite sensibly pointed out that
they were not so arrogant as to assume they knew
what was best for resources and people far away. That's
the crux of the argument the ranchers lost.

The discussion with the dissenting ranchers, as
Phillips describes it, went a little like this. The ranchers
were told that "the national voice had spoken loudly in
support of wolf reintroduction." Fine, the ranchers
replied, "if city folks want wolves, then you should
release the critters in their backyards." They were not
pleased, Phillips notes, "when I pointed out that the
nation's backyard was Yellowstone National Park."

It may be useful to define the extent of America's
backyard.

Yellowstone is surrounded by seven national forests
in Wyoming, Montana, and Idaho. There are also three
national wildlife preserves near the park, as well as several wilderness areas that exclude roads and mecha-
nized travel. Some conservationists contend that this is

the largest natural intact ecosystem on earth. Some say it's the largest in the northern hemisphere. In any case, it is a big chunk of land.

It was revered bear researcher John Craighead who began using the term Greater Yellowstone Ecosystem (GYE) in the 1960s. In 1987 the Greater Yellowstone Coordinating Committee (a cooperative Forest Service and Park Service Group) defined GYE as just under 12 million acres, while a citizens' advocacy group, the Greater Yellowstone Coalition (let's hear sustained applause), defined it as nearly double that, according to the National Park Handbook for Yellowstone.

Whether a person can live with the definition or not, the Greater Yellowstone Ecosystem, generously characterized, encompasses 43,750 square *miles.* Is that bigger than Rhode Island? Of course it is. It's also bigger than thirteen other states and the District of Colombia. It is only 8,000 square miles smaller than all of England, and nearly three times the size of Switzerland.

That's some backyard.

Every year millions of us gather at Old Faithful, the fountain on our property, in the backyard. It's fine to bump shoulders with others and watch Old Faithful blow, but I've also walked to Observation Point, a little less than a mile north, to see the eruption. One night late last October, when I wanted a little privacy, I put on a headlamp and walked up to Observation

Point to see an eruption or two under the light of a full moon. It was an experience I enjoyed in utter privacy.

There are, of course, many other places in the park where you can see untrammeled thermal features. The Brimstone Basin is all the way to hell and gone out the southeast arm of Yellowstone Lake. It seems to be little visited, but even features reasonably close to Old Faithful are not too crowded and are pleasant to visit. It just takes a little walking to get to them.

Artists' Paintpots

THERE IS A PULL-OFF ON THE GRAND LOOP A little south of Norris, and a sign directing you to Artists' Paintpots. It is a short, mostly level half-mile walk that gains some altitude at Paintpot Hill.

If the geysers inspire awe—and they do—the paintpots generally make people laugh. They are the comedians in the pantheon of thermal features. Nathaniel Langford thought the mud in the pots looked like "thick paint." He wrote that in the pots a "bubble would explode with a puff, emitting . . . a villainous smell." He didn't say that while some of the bubbles burst like boiling water, rather soundlessly, others break in a flatulent manner, creating a sound that invariably makes people laugh. You might be the world's most sophisticated individual—it won't matter. You'll still laugh when the mud pot farts.

The trail goes under some electrical wire strung up on poles—where'd that come from?—then proceeds slightly uphill. Steam rises out of a few holes in the ground, where water sloshes around deep inside. These fumaroles—I'm sorry about the nature of the extended metaphor here—sound like a giant's toilet constantly flushing itself. A vague odor of rotten eggs colors the air in the vicinity of the fumaroles.

Now geysers and fumaroles and mud pots all exist because of the molten rock seething just under the surface of the land, in the bowl of the hotspot's martini glass, if you will. Rain and snowmelt percolate below the surface. This water becomes superheated and rises, as hot water will, toward the surface. It wants to be steam, but the pressure of the earth in various narrow columns and chimneys won't let it. In those places where the earth opens above, the water flashes to steam and explodes into the air.

This is how geysers work.

Fumaroles, *Lonely Planet Yellowstone* says, are essentially dry geysers "bursting with heat but without a major water source, whose water boils away without reaching the surface." In other words, these are thirsty geysers whose eruptions happen underground. What you see on the surface are odd-shaped holes in the ground, belching steam. Fumaroles may flush or roar, and when they roar, the sound is like that of a high wind approaching. They also burp out a lot of hydrogen sulfide, that rotten-egg smell that Nathaniel Langford found so "villainous."

Mud pots, says *Lonely Planet Yellowstone,* are "created when rock is dissolved by the sulfuric acid in groundwater to create . . . a form of clay." The pots are colored by dissolved minerals, mostly iron and sulfur.

A boardwalk winds through these thermal features, taking you directly past some of the best mud pots. One pond of mud looks like a very thick stew, all chalky gray and bubbling merrily away as steam and gas rise to the surface. The mud bubbles burst with the precise sound a human makes when relieving himself of gas. There are dozens of bubbles, all bursting at once and all throwing up dribs and drabs of color.

The boardwalk then heads downhill, into a small basin. Small thermal streams run this way and that, fed by hot springs, which are composed of superheated water that rises to the surface without benefit of eruption. The hot pools, like the mud pots, derive their delicate colors—emerald green, cobalt blue—from dissolved minerals.

Then you are in the Artists' Paintpots, where more than half a dozen ponds full of colorful clay appear to boil flatulently. If an artist were to use these colors, he'd compose a picture in rusty reds and cornflower blues and chalky grays.

On my last trip to these mud pots, a few other visitors strolled about the boardwalk, nudging one another and making jokes about the bathroom sounds. Then they were gone, and I was alone with the mud pots for over an hour, thinking about artists and hotspots as well as flatulence and the end of civilization as we know it.

Monument Geyser Basin

THIS IS THE ONLY "BASIN" I KNOW THAT requires a stiff uphill climb. The trailhead is located on the west side of the Gibbon River, at the Gibbon River pull-off.

A sign reads ATTENTION HIKERS, and continues in a merry manner: WE STRONGLY RECOMMEND HIKING IN PARTIES OF 3 OR MORE PEOPLE AND STAYING ON MAINTAINED TRAILS. Hiking off-trail INCREASES THE RISK OF ENCOUNTERING BEARS. And then, just in case the visitor hasn't taken the point, the sign reads, in HUGE letters, THERE IS NO GUARANTEE OF YOUR SAFETY. The admonition concludes, IF YOU ARE UNCOMFORTABLE WITH THIS SITUATION, YOU MAY CHOOSE TO HIKE ELSEWHERE.

About twenty yards farther on the visitor is confronted by yet another sign that suggests, IF YOU ENCOUNTER A BEAR, STAY CALM. DO NOT RUN. Easy to say, more difficult to accomplish. MANY CHARGES, the sign advises, ARE BLUFF CHARGES. This seems to imply that, on occasion, bears charge with deadly intent.

One day I came upon a young couple standing there, studying the sign, as if memorizing the suggestion that, in the face of a charging bear, one might want to SLOWLY DETOUR OR BACK AWAY. If a bear attacks, victims are advised to PLAY DEAD. DROP TO THE GROUND, LIFT YOUR LEGS TO YOUR CHEST, AND CLASP YOUR HANDS OVER THE BACK OF YOUR NECK. WEARING YOUR PACK WILL SHIELD YOUR BODY. Especially if it's one of those bulletproof Kevlar ones.

The young couple and I exchanged greetings. They were, it turned out, from Virginia and quite familiar with black bears. When they learned that I lived in the area, they asked me about grizzly bears. I told them the truth, that I'd seen quite a few, some from the safety of a vehicle, some while I was on foot. The bears I'd seen while on foot were always a goodly distance away, and I'd never feared greatly for my life.

As we walked along, we passed one more sign, apparently posted for the dullest of the dull, the ones who simply refuse to "get it." In huge letters the sign said, THERE IS NO GUARANTEE OF YOUR SAFETY WHILE HIKING OR CAMPING IN BEAR COUNTRY. The advisory continued, DON'T TRAVEL ALONE (as I had been, until I met up with the couple perusing the signs). The sign said that it was a bad idea to travel after dark and that it was wise to USE CAUTION WHERE VISION IS OBSTRUCTED. Some of the advice seemed fairly self-evident: AVOID BEARS WHEN SEEN. Good thinking. NEVER APPROACH OR ATTEMPT TO FEED BEARS. I could do that.

The three of us decided that the signs themselves were almost as scary as the possibility of a marauding bear. This was our way of whistling past the graveyard. WHEN CAMPING, the sign continued, DON'T CAMP IN AREAS FREQUENTED BY BEARS. D'oh! DON'T CARRY OR USE ODOROUS FOODS. Other advice included: SLEEP 100 YARDS FROM FOOD STORAGE AND COOKING AREAS. . . . USE A TREE TO HANG ALL FOOD, COOKING GEAR, AND TOI-LETRIES: HANG THIS STUFF TEN FEET UP AND FOUR FEET FROM THE TRUNK OF THE TREE. . . . WHEN FISHING, DIS-POSE OF THE ENTRAILS OF THE FISH BY PUNCTURING ITS AIR BLADDER AND THROWING THE GUTS INTO DEEP WATER.

One bit of information was not entirely obvious on its face: AVOID CARCASSES; BEARS OFTEN DEFEND THIS SOURCE OF FOOD.

This sign reminded me of a bear-and-carcass story. I related it to the couple as we passed the final signs and walked the flat part of the trail at the edge of Gib-bon Meadows. I told them about the time I fell asleep while watching a grizzly that was less than 200 yards away. There was a carcass involved in the story as well.

This is the way it happened. I voluntarily went with a friend to watch a grizzly bear feast on the carcass of something that had once been a bison. This was off trail, out in the Hayden Valley, over on the other side of the Great Loop. The bear was in a small dell—call it a basin—in the middle of a huge Yellowstone meadow, very like the one the couple and I could see from the trail, Gibbon Meadows. As in Gibbon, there were almost no trees to climb in the Hayden Valley. My friend Tom Murphy (who makes an appearance in many of my Yellowstone experiences) had been out "dinking around" the day before. About four in the afternoon he spotted a grizzly feeding on the carcass of an adult bison. At sunset it began assiduously digging a hole. The muscular hump on the grizzly's back powered this steam-shovel action of its front legs. It took very little time—a matter of minutes—for the bear to bury the bison and cover it over with loose dirt. Tom knew his bear would dig the bison up the next day and feed again.

That night he asked me if I wanted to go back up to the park to watch this culinary whoop-dee-do. I did, I really wanted to see it, but bears scare me badly, and I didn't sleep at all that night. Not a wink. It hardly mattered because we were up well before dawn and had parked at a turn-off in the Hayden Valley very early indeed. The valley had once been an arm of Yellowstone Lake. Over the centuries very fine silt and clay were deposited on the lake bottom so that when the water retreated, the soil was almost impermeable, and very few trees grow there as a consequence. So, for instance, if you go there to see a ravenous grizzly bear devour the remains of the largest land animal in North America, you have no place to hide. There are no trees to climb. You are out in the open—and out of luck if the bear's charge isn't a bluff.

Tom and I walked toward this bear, moving over marshy hillocks that sometimes quivered like jelly under our boots. We walked five miles, at a guess, through a herd of rutting bison, then dropped and belly-crawled the last few hundred yards until we came to the small indentation in the earth. Our only cover was a stand of sagebrush, maybe two and a half feet high. We hid there, upwind of the bear below, and I trembled in my parka.

In this bear pit was a hole that looked like a big freshly dug grave. At sunrise the bear, which had been sleeping nearby, dug into the grave for a while, reached down, and with one paw—one paw!—flipped the bison up out of the hole and dropped it beside the grave. The carcass had to weigh well over a thousand pounds. The bear had buried it there for safekeeping.

The grizzly began eating. He was an older male, with long white claws, and was obviously the boss bear in the neighborhood. No one challenged him for his meat, even though dozens of lesser bears must have smelled the carcass. Our griz ate for hours: he ate until his stomach became visibly distended. At about noon, in the heat of the day, he climbed into the empty grave, which must have been cooler, and took a nap. All I could see of him was his silly-looking bear-nose pointing up at the sky and a great curve of distended bear-belly projecting out of the hole.

Because I'd spent an entirely sleepless night, slumber beckoned. It was almost seductive. I could feel my eyelids flicker. After an hour of watching the bear sleep, I myself—this is hard to admit—I myself fell asleep no more than 200 yards from a grizzly bear.

I told my new friends about this incident as if it were a joke. It was supposed to be a funny story, but the young couple did not laugh. Rather they regarded me in a silent and suspicious manner. I am not sure whether they thought I was a moron or a liar. In any case, we continued on, trudging along silently.

Relatively few people visit Monument Geyser Basin, but not, I think, because of all the signs warning of bears. There are many such signs located in dozens of "bear frequenting" areas in the park. No, the reason you can often have Monument Geyser Basin to yourself is because it is a stiff uphill climb, rising 640 feet in about half a mile. People would rather be mauled by a bear that take a stiff forty-five-minute uphill hike, or so it would seem.

The first half-mile or so, before the trail turns uphill, we all looked out into Gibbon Meadows, where the deer and the antelope play. Actually, I've never seen an antelope in Gibbon Meadows and doubt they exist there. The antelope is the fastest animal in North America: they've been clocked at speeds up to 60 miles per hour. They naturally prefer open fields and meadows—in such places they can see for miles and simply outrun any approaching predator.

What probably limited the antelope in the area is that this meadow of the Gibbon River, like the Hayden Valley, is full of little hillocks of marshy ground. It's a bad track for a fast antelope. These speed demons can't put the pedal to the metal on ground that quivers like jelly under the foot. Or more properly, under the hoof.

The fact is, at Gibbon Meadows, hikers who are not busy encountering bears are more likely to see herds of elk and bison. Sometime there are moose. Late in the day sandhill cranes can often be heard making their eerie "loon on amphetamines" call. It sounds a bit like ululations of Arab women at war, that odd thing they do with their tongues.

This is what I especially like about Yellowstone: the conjunction of meadow and mountain. It is a place where wildlife congregates. Part of the reason Yellowstone is the Serengeti Plain of North America is that all the creatures of the plain and the mountain converge in this landscape of marvels, a wonderland originally preserved solely for its thermal features. Back in 1872 no one knew that wildlife itself would eventually become so scarce that some folks would value it even more highly than all the thermal features contained in the park.

The couple and I walked along the trail to Monument Geyser Basin, which moves parallel to the immense meadow for half a mile or so. Nearby fumaroles howled and flushed, belching out their distinctive villainous odor. We turned left and began the uphill grade that led to a long narrow basin filled with fumaroles and bubbling thermal ponds. The fires of 1988 had been particularly fierce near the basin, and whole forests of standing dead trees, either charred black or weathered gray, leaned against one another at odd angles.

The eponymous Monument Geyser, which looks a bit like a Thermos bottle and is often called Thermal Bottle Geyser, is ten feet high. The cone of the geyser was formed from silica, rock dissolved in the molten bowels below Yellowstone, and then deposited with the erupting waters on the surface of the earth. Monument Geyser steams a bit and splashes some water, but most of the odd-shaped cones in the basin are inactive. Roger and Carol Anderson, in *Yellowstone Day Hikes,* write that "through the years, people have conceived of the most unusual images in these sinter (formed of silica) cones, giving them names like Sunning Seal, the Dog's Head, and the Sperm Whale."

The young couple and I tried to pick out Dog's Head and Sperm Whale, but most everything looked more or less like a sunning seal. The woman was the best of us: she saw alligators and penguins and ducks and Oprah Winfrey. Soon enough the couple decided they'd had enough. I elected to stay.

There was a symphony in progress. Fumaroles were providing a constant bass, a roaring that played like the soundtrack of every documentary you've ever seen on Antarctica. Meanwhile, in a minor key, I listened to the sound of gently bubbling boiling water and the burble of a thermal spring, all interspersed with various birdcalls and the sigh of the wind though burned timber.

The standing dead trees were silhouetted against perfectly blue sky. Those that had weathered the most were the color of tarnished pewter. Some still sported a few fire-shortened branches, twisted against the sky like arthritic fingers raised in supplication. Others were charcoal black and had lost all their branches. They leaned at odd angles, and many of them had lost their shape to the fire so that they looked like ebony totem poles, fire-scorched in such a way that one could see in them a screaming mouth, a tortured face, and empty burned-out eyes.

I stayed alone in the basin for hours, listening to the symphony, examining the geyser cones, and contemplating the burned-out forest, all of which I thought of as the Art Out of Hell.

Ice Lake

O N THE WAY FROM NORRIS TO CANYON VIL-
lage, up near the top of a hill, there is pull-out
to Ice Lake and camp 4D3. What I particularly like
about this very short walk is that Ice Lake camp 4D3 is
totally wheelchair accessible. There is a boardwalk
across the ditch by the side of the road, and the
smooth wide dirt track is suitable for wheelchairs. I
doubt if the camp is more than a quarter of a mile
from the road. It has a handicapped-accessible toilet,
appropriate tent sites, and a wonderful view of blue
and frigid-looking Ice Lake.

I strolled out around the lake, thinking about
America. Is this a great country or what? Where else
would the wilderness—or one lovely part of it, anyway—be made accessible in such a way that the dis-
abled can spend entire sleepless nights worried about
being eaten by a bear, just like any able-bodied hiker?

The trail continued around the lake. The firestorm of 1988 was very fierce there. In places at the north end of the lake, for instance, I saw fallen dead trees more than two and three and sometimes four deep, forming a raggedy sort of fence. Someone—a ranger, of course—had done an awful lot of work with a chain saw just to make the trail walkable.

I was going toward Grebe Lake, but a sign at the Ice Lake trailhead had said that this was a bad idea: there were bears frequenting Grebe Lake at the moment. Never mind. I didn't have to come out at Grebe Lake. Bill Schneider's *Best Easy Day Hikes Yellowstone* had informed me of a nifty shortcut that would let me avoid Grebe Lake altogether and drop me on the road about half a mile above my car. I had to ford the Little Gibbon River, which might have been a problem early in the year, but it was late September and the water was low. I just stepped across on the rocks.

My problem was that it was getting dark. I needed to move. I had a headlamp—I always carry one—but I didn't want to be out in bear country after dark. The trail was a little hard to find in the twilight, and I was moving through stands of silvery burned trees, many of which had fallen. New lodgepole pine, some of them twelve feet high, grew in the interstices of the ghost forest, so that there was a riot of green against the high silver of the decimated trees.

The trail dropped down to the Little Gibbon River. There was another ford, a steep rise, and then I found myself looking down at a small waterfall on the river. It was a fall I'd never heard about, hidden away in a corner of sculpted yellow rock. Other people had certainly seen this fall. It was close to the road, after all, but it was well off the main trail, and here it was, cascading over slick rock, as if for me alone. I felt something expand inside my chest.

There followed a time when I didn't know exactly where I was—lost in my own backyard again—but I could hear cars out on the highway and headed in that direction through a large meadow where one bull elk herded twenty cows in studly self-importance. His antlers were huge, as if he were some 1950s tough guy with a pompadour. Twenty cows! What a stud! Then he bugled: a sound that echoes across meadow and forest, that keeps cows in line, that challenges all comers, that sends chills up a human's spine, and that nonetheless sounds like a combination squeak and squeal. Frankly, it sounds sort of dorky coming out of such a majestic animal.

The Grand Canyon
of the Yellowstone

THE GRAND CANYON OF THE YELLOWSTONE and the 308-foot-high Lower Falls of the Yellowstone River are two of the attractions that surely moved early visitors to the area to think in terms of national park. The canyon itself is 800 to 1,200 feet deep and 24 miles long. The upper two and a half miles are the most colorful. Generally people drive from viewpoint to viewpoint, but you can hike the trail, which is not particularly salubrious in that it parallels the road in many places and you wonder why you're there. In fact, no one in their right mind would walk the trail.

Still, you do come upon the odd and unexpected. From the brink of the Lower Falls, for instance, you could take the North Rim Trail and cross Cascade Creek on a wooden bridge. The trail rises. About 100 yards farther, look back. What you see is Cascade

Creek Falls, which is about 70 feet high. It's difficult to imagine that you're the only person who has ever seen this fall since there is traffic noise in the distance and boot tracks in the mud below, but on many days you will be the only person contemplating Cascade Creek Falls, and that is a gift.

On the south rim of the Grand Canyon, there is a nice stiff hike down to the bottom of Uncle Tom's Trail. In the very early 1900s, so says a sign, "Uncle" Tom Richardson took visitors down into the canyon on a series of stairs and rope ladders. The trail now descends about three-quarters of the way into the canyon, down 328 metal steps. The climb is not recommended for those suffering from heart or breathing problems.

The view of the Lower Falls is worth the walk. At the top of the fall is a V of neon-green water, and rock rises on either side another 100 or so feet. Watching the fall is like watching a fire: the same thing keeps happening and happening but just a little differently every time, so that it holds the eye and empties the mind. The effect is hypnotic. The green streak in the fall fades about a third of the way down. Spray rises from the pool at the base of the fall like smoke from a fire, and the thunder of falling water echoes as the mist freezes on the yellow and pink mineralized walls of the canyon. The mist below, stirred by the wind, moves swiftly and seems impossibly clean, entirely pristine.

The South Rim Trail proceeds downstream from the top of Uncle Tom's Staircase to Artist Point, which, you will see as you emerge from the trees, is a crowded parking lot. Walk to the observation point and look downstream. Rock pinnacles on the steep canyon slopes—whole busy cities of them—run red down to the water below. Osprey nest in the trees that somehow cling to ledges, and the colors deepen as the sun drops lower in the sky. Below, steam rises from thermal features and looks pink against the canyon wall. The river, at this place, pours over several small terraces and flows out into a series of emerald-green pools.

Some of the opposite wall is positively sulfurous in color, and much of it is peaked up in pinkish rock that looks red in the fading light of late afternoon. Soon it will be dark. It's rather like reading a great book by candlelight: just when you get to the good part, the candle flutters and dies.

I walked the South Rim Trail alone in the twilight. I had my headlamp on, although I didn't absolutely need it. It was dark in the trees, but the clouds were lit from below, crimson, as from the light of distant fires. I thought of the view from Artist Point. When the artist Thomas Moran, of the Hayden party, wrote about this view (or one very close), he said, "its beautiful tints were beyond the reach of human art." Which didn't stop him from trying to convey it. His massive painting of the Grand Canyon of the Yellowstone (composed a bit downstream from Artist Point) hangs in the Smithsonian today. Some say this monumental work had a strong effect on Congress back in the 1870s—people who saw it were inclined to preserve the area. In any case, despite the artist's protestation that he was unequal to the project, his painting had a great deal to do with formulating the "best idea America ever had."

I wandered back to my car in a funk. The words of Ferdinand Hayden rang all too true: "No language can do justice to the wonderful grandeur and beauty of the canyon." Which didn't stop him from trying. Me either, for that matter.

The Lamar Valley

IN MY OPINION, IT IS WORTH GETTING OFF THE Grand Loop in order to see the Lamar Valley, in the northeast quarter of the park. This immense sage-littered valley stretches out in an explosion of wildlife. Odd thermal features throw up steam in the distance, and this is most easily seen in the winter.

The Lamar is at its best in winter. It is the lowest and warmest area of the park, which means the animals come down from the high country and congregate not so very far from the road. Great herds of elk and bison move through the snow. The road through this wonderland is the only one in the park that is open all year long.

Several years ago there were reportedly more coyotes in the Lamar Valley than any other place on earth. That may not be so these days. About half the coyotes have been killed by the gray wolves that were reintroduced to the park in 1995. The dead coyotes are the ones that stood their ground and battled the wolves for the kill. They were what the biologists call "naïve" and what the rest of us would describe as "dead." The surviving coyotes have learned a lesson. They'll still try to steal wolf kill, but they do it by stealth. No confrontations.

I watched an attempt at such thievery one day near the pull-off by Druid Peak. Okay, I wasn't walking; I was on cross-country skis with half a dozen of my friends. It's the principle of the thing, anyway: we were moving, not sitting in our cars eating doughnuts.

The Druid Peak pack was then the biggest, strongest, meanest wolf pack in the park. The pack has recently declined and fallen, rather like the Roman Empire. It's in the nature of wolf packs, I guess, as well as empires.

In any case, the wolves of Druid Peak were at the pinnacle of their success this winter day. They must have killed something. I was skiing on a track near the road, and when I looked up toward Druid Peak, I could see wolves plainly moving around up there. Ravens circled above, signifying a carcass. Several coyotes were working their way up to the peak, carefully keeping their heads turned to one side, as if they really weren't walking up the hill with the intention of stealing some meat from the kill. The coyotes yipped and barked as if signaling one another. There were three of them to the south and four others on the ridge to the west. It was about midday.

The wolves were moving slowly through the snow, then one by one they lay down. They had been feeding all morning, and now it was nap time. This is typical wolf behavior: the animals gorge and then fall into a deep sleep. Scientists say that such wolves are "meat drunk."

The meat drunk moment was the one the coyotes, no longer naïve, had been waiting for. They moved in on the kill, which was hidden up there on the other side of the peak. Nothing happened for some time. Suddenly all seven coyotes came out from behind the ridge at a dead run and leaped over a hill so steep, some might call it a cliff. They ran and slipped and slid down the hill, running for their very lives. I'd never, ever seen any coyote move that fast.

Then, high above, a huge majestic silver gray wolf came slowly strolling over the top of the hill. He stared down at the fleeing coyotes and seemed to nod, as if all were right with the world. He sat at the base of a tree and looked down at the coyotes and the herds of humans and elk and bison. He was the lord of all he surveyed, and life was good.

Now that may be an entirely anthropomorphic interpretation, and I apologize for it. However, let me say with complete accuracy that this wolf-and-coyote show has enlivened and brightened my existence since I saw it, and when I cast back to that moment and think about the silver gray wolf near the top of Druid Peak, it is easy to believe that life is good.

Fossil Forest

*I*F YOU WANT TO SEE A PETRIFIED TREE—AND
who doesn't?—get off the Grand Loop at Tower
Junction, in the northeast part of the park, and drive
east. There is a sign and a turn-off that leads to a parking area. The tree in question is about a three-minute
walk along a paved path. It is a pillar of stone about 25
feet high, a former redwood tree, bleached and stained
like an old statue, but one that seems to have the exact
texture of wood. It is surrounded by a green picket
fence, like a grave, and the last time I was there two
dozen people stood jostling one another, shoving for
the best angle to shoot photos or video. Not a single
person was actually looking at the tree. They were
looking at it through lenses.

Somehow this depressed me. No matter. I was on
my way to see some petrified trees with a couple of
friends of mine, Toby Undem and Matt Smith. None

of us had made this walk before. It was supposed to be short but steep. The trail head was unmarked, the trail itself unmaintained. We'd have the trees to ourselves if we could find them.

The walk starts at a pull-off about 5.3 miles east of Tower Junction on the way into the wildlife paradise of the Lamar Valley. About 1,200 feet above, through several stands of Douglas fir, there are whole forests that have been turned to stone. More than 200 plant species have been identified, and some of them carry the mind off into a wet subtropical past that is difficult to visualize. There are fossilized breadfruit and avocado trees, magnolia and dogwood, as well as redwood, maple, oak, and hickory. Fossil forests exist atop earlier fossil forests.

It happened like this: about 50 million years ago the area was—you'll excuse the expression—a hotbed of volcanic activity. This volcanism was totally unrelated to the much later events that formed Yellowstone as we know it today and that we already considered while on the summit of Mount Washburn. No, these were just some old volcanoes spewing out the usual flow of light ash and gas and water and sand. As this volcanic froth poured down the mountainsides, whole forests were buried from the ground to the crown. Before the buried trees could rot, silica, the dissolved rock in the volcanic flow, plugged the living cells of the trees, creating forests of stone.

But volcanic soils are fertile, which explains why humans have always made their homes in the shadows of dormant and active volcanoes. Stuff grows in volcanic soils, and in Yellowstone whole new forests grew up on top of the buried forests, sometimes in as little as 200 years. And then these forests were buried themselves in yet another eruption. Geologists suggest that volcanism created as many as 27 separate fossil forests on or around Specimen Ridge.

"Yellowstone contains so many wonders, the fact that is has the largest petrified forest in the world goes almost unnoticed," say Roger and Carol Anderson in *A Ranger's Guide to Yellowstone Day Hikes.* I, on the other hand, have been consumed by the concept of fossil forests since I first heard about them. I can't really wrap my mind around the concept: 50-million-year-old trees, some still standing, sculpted in stone. Folk tales, told by old-time explorers and trappers, are colorful and perfectly unilluminating, at least in the scientific sense.

Yarn-spinning mountain man Jim Bridger poked around in what is now the park in the early 1830s and many decades later had occasion to speak with General Nelson Miles. This was in 1897. As recounted by Aubrey Haines in *The Yellowstone Story,* the General asked Bridger if he'd ever been as far south as Zuni, New Mexico.

"No, thar ain't any beaver down thar."

"But Jim, there are some things in this world besides beaver. I was down there last winter and saw great trees with limbs and bark all turned into stone."

"O," returned Jim, "that's peetrification. Come with me to the Yellowstone and I'll show you peetrified trees a-growing with peetrified birds on 'em a-singing peetrified songs."

Another Bridger tale, this time recounted by Hiram Chittenden in *The Yellowstone National Park* (1895), notes that petrifications in the northeast corner of the park, on Specimen Ridge, probably provided the "base material" out of which Bridger "contrived" what Chittenden calls a "picturesque yarn." In this tale, a "great medicine man of the Crow nation" cursed a certain mountain. Neither Chittenden nor Bridger say what the shaman had against the mountain. He just cursed it. That's all. And "everything upon the mountain at the time of this dire event became instantly petrified and has remained so ever since. All forms of life are standing about in stone where they were suddenly caught by the petrifying influences." At this point, Bridger's tale veers off on a flight of almost shivery fancy: "Sage brush, grass, prairie fowl, antelope, elk and bears may be seen as perfect as in actual life. Even flowers are blooming in colors of crystal, and birds soar with wings spread in motionless flight, while the air floats with music and perfumes siliceous, and the sun and moon shine with petrified light."

I think that's the best petrification story. Bridger was justly famous for his tall tales, and Captain W. F. Raynolds, who had Bridger for a guide in 1859 and 1860, suggested that men like Jim Bridger who lacked the comforts and culture of civilization would, of necessity, make a theater out of campfire storytelling and "beguile the monotony of camp life by 'spinning yarns' in which each tried to excel all others."

Bridger won. Historian Haines goes to great lengths to dig up all the tall tales of woodsmen describing petrified forests previous to Bridger's accounts. There were many over the years, often retold by educated writers who rendered the backwoodsman's account in what I suspect was meant to be hilarious dialect. (Is "peetrification" funny? What about a mountain man so unacquainted with proper English that fossil forests are described as "putrifications," a word that caused listeners to inquire if the stone trees "smelled badly"?)

In any case, Aubrey Haines reliably gets to the bottom of the various putrifactions and comes to the conclusion that "if lying was one of Bridger's sins—as some have hinted—it was seldom *original* sin; he has had willing collaborators." What Haines means, I think, is that, over the past 150 years or so, certain writers have quoted Bridger as if the image of birds petrified in flight sprang from his lips in the manner that poems flowed from Lord Byron's pen. Haines seems a bit put out by this. He wants facts. Me, I just like a good story, and this one was told and retold in front of camp-fires over the years until Jim Bridger was able to build upon the tale and make it his own in all its fantastic and memorable glory. As I say, Bridger won.

I was thinking about this as Toby, Matt, and I left our car and walked off on the vague path that I thought to be the fossil forest trail. I was encouraged that both my companions felt that if there was any track at all, we were on it. I'd put this hike together and was respon-sible for getting us to stone trees high above.

Ahead of us, a herd of about 60 bison was slowly grazing its way east. We took a wide turn and tried to put a couple of hundred yards between us and the buffalo. The valley floor was very nearly flat, covered over in grasses and sparse sage. Suddenly something spooked the bison. It wasn't us, because they turned back and were running in our direction. Their trajec-tory took them about 100 yards north of us. We could feel the ground rumble under our feet.

"Well," Toby said, "that was exciting."

I wondered what it must have felt like when the great herds of bison ruled the plains. If 60 of the beasts made the ground rumble, what was the sound of 100,000 stampeding?

The trail, such as it is, crosses the valley floor and rises into some trees. The forest is thick and dark and there are many paths. The guide books say to stay on the steepest of them, that the others are "social trails" made by pilgrims looking for an easy way to get to the stone trees. The easy trails would not get us where we wanted to go. And so I trudged on as the trail got progressively steeper and the forest closed in darkly around us.

It was early fall, and dozens of squirrels were dashing about overhead, intent on their hectic squirrel business. Occasionally one would dash to a high branch and scold us with a quick and constant chattering sound. In fact, there was a whole line of squirrels behind us and several in front of us, chattering and scolding. They were chronicling our progress through the trees. I stopped to listen. Were the squirrels scolding us, or was the scolding out ahead, moving in our direction? If so, it would not be a good thing.

Squirrels probably scold humans because we look like bears. In the fall, bears go into an orgy of feeding to prepare for hibernation. They gorge on things like white-pine cone nuts. Now anyone who has ever tried to get a nut out of a white-pine cone knows that it takes time and some fine motor skills. So the bears let squirrels do the scut work. Once the squirrel has stashed his nuts for the fall, the hungry bear finds them and gobbles them up. Consequently, squirrels dislike bears intensely.

All of which means that it is wise to take precautions when a severe treetop scolding is heading your way.

But the squirrels were only scolding the three of

us—nothing else—as we labored through the steeply sloping forest. Eventually we came out on a rather flat rocky plateau that was scattered with small rocks that may have been the remains of a fossil forest. A few rocks looked like big logs, and that's what they were, the shattered remains of several fallen stone trees.

Toby and Matt expressed the opinion that we may have come up too steeply and somehow missed the standing fossils. This seemed to be my fault.

I suggested we climb a bit more, and then I found a path that side-hilled its way through another dark forest. These stone trees were tricky. The damn things had been standing in the same place for 50 million years, but I couldn't find them. Presently we saw a light at the end of the darkness. The forest fell away. And there it was.

The standing stump of ancient redwood was about 5 feet high and 26 feet in diameter. It was possible to see the pattern the tree's bark had formed in life all those millions of years ago. The slope on which the stump stood was eroding, which is how the forests had become exposed. Underneath the tree, where the ground had fallen away, there were stone roots snaking into the earth. Below, two other standing fossilized trees stood sentinel. Matt Smith, whose business is constructing dinosaurs for museums and exhibits, explained the geology to me and, as usual, I found myself more confused than ever. He used words like "conglomerate" and "tuft" and "mudstone." In any case, the way the stone lay proved to Matt that the redwoods below were fossilized in a separate and earlier volcanic event.

"Right," I said. We sat at the base of the big redwood and ate our lunches. There was no forest below, not on this side of the slope, and we could see a new, easier path down the hill. Two small herds of bison grazed on the valley floor and, not far away, a perfectly blue glacial lake glittered in the sun.

"This hike was a good idea," Matt said, and Toby agreed with him. I stared down at the valley. "Yeah," I said, "these trees are something." I was experiencing one of my truly rare moments of extremely high self-esteem. "Petrified trees," I thought, rephrasing the immortal Joe Louis, "they can hide but they can't run."

IN THE BACKCOUNTRY
THREE GOOD BACKCOUNTRY TREKS

Of the thousand or more miles of trail in Yellowstone Park, I've decided to describe three backcountry treks encompassing only a couple hundred miles. I won't even mention various off-trail destinations favored by persons like my friend Doug Peacock, author of Grizzly Years. *Doug sort of smiles indulgently when I ask him if he's been on this trail or that. "I don't go on trails," he explains.*

I, on the other hand, with my hopeless sense of direction, generally stay on a trail and bushwhack out around my campsite. That's what I did a few years ago, with my friend Tom Murphy. We'd been hired to write up these trips for National Geographic Adventure *magazine. Here is a chronicle of three of those trips, updated, revised, and greatly expanded.*

Into the Throrofare

*A*LOT OF STRANGE AND WONDROUS THINGS ARE happening in the largely unknown backcountry of Yellowstone. The park is big—bigger, in fact, than some states: about 2.22 million acres, with 97 trail-heads and at least a thousand miles of trail, as well as great expanses of land that aren't served by any trails at all. A man might spend a lifetime walking the back-country and never know it all. This means there is always something to discover. But discovering some-thing is one thing; beating one's chest about it is quite another.

For example:

In *The Guide to Yellowstone Waterfalls and Their Dis-covery,* by Paul Rubinstein, Lee Whittlesey, and Mike Stevens, published in 2000, the authors report that they "discovered" 240 unknown, unmapped, or unpho-tographed waterfalls. No kidding? In this day and age, new discoveries! Well, not precisely. A foreword, by Dr. Judith Myer, puts the matter in perspective: "The title of 'discoverer' is not necessarily bestowed on someone who sees something for the first time. A discoverer discloses information to others," in the manner, for instance, that Christopher Columbus discovered America.

This is not an evil, nor even a fraudulent book. The authors may have truly found some unseen water. Maybe. But they themselves acknowledge that a few "privileged" individuals "did see some" of the waterfalls. "Most of them, however, failed to write reports . . . or photograph them, or even map them" and therefore "missed their chance at credit for their discoveries."

In fact, many hundreds of Boy Scouts had seen at least one of these falls before, and rangers, seeking to limit erosion, had built a trail to one of them. But it was the authors who publicized the "find," and they beat out the Boy Scouts fair and square.

Furthermore, some of those privileged individuals who had seen various falls previously, it must be said, missed their chance to be called "discoverers" in the name of what I can only describe as the their interest in the preservation of wonder. Indeed, certain rangers, guides, and knowledgeable hikers find the concept of credit for discovery disagreeable. The authors themselves note that "some wilderness advocates hate the idea of official names in wilderness areas and love the idea of large spaces on the maps where there are no names."

That was the gist of the argument that swirled about the *Waterfalls* book on the fringes of Yellowstone Park. It was a low-level dispute: no one doubted the authors' hard work or honesty or good intentions, only the wisdom of their catalog approach to wilderness. Others, generally outside the area, just read the headlines. Friends and colleagues called from New York, thrilled about the 240 new waterfalls.

Which, the authors said, was part of the plan: "We hope the revelation of these beautiful natural features will spur city dwellers, who need these places for mental health and restoration more than anyone else"—nutcases!—"to use their resources to protect them by voting for environmental candidates rather than developers, by yelling loudly whenever there are threats to these places." And so on, in admirable open-handed altruism.

It occurred to me that if these three guys could spend seven summers searching for waterfalls on behalf of the sanity of city dwellers everywhere, the least I could do for the pitiable urbanites of my acquaintance was to spend a lot of time selflessly hiking the backcountry with my friends. I'd let the water fall where it may, and later we could all go out and yell at some developers together.

Hiking Yellowstone, out of sight of any road, seems to be on everyone's unfulfilled wish list. It is often said that 99 percent of the visitors to Yellowstone never see the backcountry. Out of curiosity, I checked this out and found that this statistic is somewhat understated. In 2001, according to Yellowstone Visitor Services, there were 2,758,526 recreational visitors, of whom 19,239 applied for a backcountry camping permit. That means—rounding the numbers off a bit—that in 2001 a full 99.3 percent of park visitors didn't overnight in the backcountry.

I am, myself, a good bad example. I have lived just 50 miles north of the park for twenty-five years, and until a few years ago, I could count the number of my overnight backcountry trips on the fingers of one hand, a shameful statistic in itself. Another reason to get out on the trail.

As it happens, my neighbor, photographer Tom Murphy, has been a guide in Yellowstone for the past eighteen years and knows it as well as anyone of my acquaintance. Together we planned several runs into the park. I'd write about our trips for publication. Tom would take photos. It is possible to argue that we were doing all this for the mental health and restoration of others. Strange, then, that all of our planned destinations involved several days' worth of walking, an activity that both Tom and I know buys solitude in Yellowstone.

Our first trip, for instance, would lead us up over the mountains of the Bridger-Teton Wilderness Area, then into the southeast corner of Yellowstone Park, where we would pass by the Thorofare Ranger Station, 32 miles from anywhere, the most remote occupied dwelling in the contiguous United States. The second trip, which we'd both always wanted to make, would be to the Goblin Labyrinth; and in the third we'd spend some time visiting the Bechler River area, which I came to think of as the River of Reliable Rainbows.

And so, on that first trip in late July, seven of us found ourselves walking north toward the Thorofare Ranger Station, exactly 32 miles from the trailhead. The route would take us over the top of the world, the Continental Divide, at a place called Two Ocean Pass, just outside the park. The divide itself runs through a marshy bog about three miles long. Pacific Creek, which we were following to the top of the world, flows out of the bog south and west; at the north end of the bog, the watercourse flowing north and east is called Atlantic Creek. As the names suggest, these two streams, separated by only three miles, empty into entirely disparate oceans.

"So," Tom Murphy explained to me, "a fish could conceivably swim up Pacific Creek, muddle through the bog, and end up swimming down Atlantic Creek." That's why Tom wanted to walk an extra 32 miles, enduring 3,000 feet or more of elevation change, carrying his ninety-pound backpack mostly full of camera gear. He wanted to see a place where a fish could swim across the Continental Divide. Tom, I should explain, was raised on a cattle ranch in South Dakota, 60 miles from the nearest town, and is prone to become excited about concepts like fish swimming over the Rocky Mountains. This is what happens when you grow up without a television in the house.

We had started trekking in the Bridger-Teton Wilderness, trudging north, toward the border of Yellowstone Park. The meadow we reached is a mile wide and flanked by wooded hillsides. Pacific Creek runs through the middle of it. Trudging along in the series of parallel ruts made by grazing cows, seven of us stepped through an impressionist painter's wet dream of wildflowers: yellow alpine buttercups, purple asters, harebell, Queen Anne's lace, pink fireweed, blue lupin, goldenrod, mustard, interspersed with the occasional cowflop. We were moving slowly up toward the Continental Divide and the entrance to Yellowstone Park, beyond which we hoped to meet with the backcountry ranger stationed at the famously remote Thorofare Ranger Station. The cabin, as I've said, is 32 miles from the nearest road, and we had just started, so we had 32 miles to go, and then 32 more miles to get out the other way. The mosquitoes could be bad in July, not to mention the horseflies, which actually tear bits of flesh off the body. You are more likely to be bitten by a horsefly in Yellowstone than by any other creature. This is no laughing matter: horsefly bites hurt.

Then again, any one of us could also be eaten by a grizzly bear, or be butted by a two-thousand-pound bison or a fifteen-hundred-pound moose, or suffer a dehydrating bout of giardia. Alternately, a person could fall or break a leg or have a serious medical emergency 32 miles from the nearest road.

I imagine these are some of the reasons that almost no one ever visits the Yellowstone backcountry. Or it may simply be that folks just don't care to walk very far. In any case, the figures don't lie: 99.3 percent of park visitors do not overnight in the backcountry.

A day's walk or more from the border of Yellowstone, we set up our camp at the edge of the meadow and looked back, south, toward a ridge of jagged sawtoothed rock rising in the distance—the Teton range—with glaciers on the shoulders of Grand Teton and Mount Moran glittering in the late afternoon sun, stark against a perfectly blue sky.

In the morning the sun rose through high clouds to the east so that slanting pillars of light fell across the meadow, illuminating the wildflowers, the way light falls in medieval paintings of saints, and we made our way up Pacific Creek toward Two Oceans Pass. It took a couple of days, but we eventually stumbled into the bog at the top of the world. Tom Murphy and I, along with another friend, Dr. David Long, a biochemist turned fine printmaker, post-holed through the mud out into the marsh, looking for the exact spot where a fish might swim across the Continental Divide. The map said we were 8,200 feet above sea level.

The bog was about half a mile across and maybe three miles long. Its willows were thick but seldom more than waist high. Where the ground rose slightly, it was covered by profusions of purple monk's hood, a flower that looks pretty much like its name. Underfoot, slowly running copper-colored water made countless narrow furrows in the marshy ground, and these small streams—some no more than a foot wide—ran in long roundabout curving courses or in shorter dithering meanders. Tom, Dave, and I spread out, all looking for the exact place where black-spotted westslope trout might slip over the divide and into waters destined for the Atlantic. I followed a likely stream out toward the middle of the bog. It got smaller and the willows got higher so that they covered the creek, and I was obliged to probe down through the foliage with my walking stick to see if there was still water below. Presently, there wasn't.

Meanwhile, Tom found a tiny ridgeline, about two or three feet higher than the surrounding land, and stood there, in an area of rusty burned grasses about the size of a football field. Water to the west seemed to flow west; eastern waters to the east. We stood for a

strangely triumphant moment on the exact instant of
the Continental Divide and discussed transcontinental
trout.

Later in the day we pushed off to the north and
east, walking beside the outflow from the bog. Atlantic
Creek drops down through forests of burned trees,
great limbless lodgepole pine, whole forests of standing
dead, all weathered a ghostly silver white. Sometimes
the trail took us through meadows alive with every
manner of wildflower—sego lilies, for instance, which
look a bit like white tulips with round red spots on the
inner petals. Eileen Ralicke, an emergency room nurse
who was a member of our party, declared the sego lily
"the most beautiful thing I've ever seen." Kara Kreitlow, another emergency room nurse—Tom and Dave
and I weren't taking any chances, you see——agreed.

The land had risen from the west slope in a series
of stair-step meadows and now floated down to the
north and east in meadows several miles wide. Here
flowers grew in patchwork brilliance, sometimes spiraling out from a central point or covering scattered
acres here and there. This route, over Two Ocean Pass,
was the path once used by the pioneer trappers. The
trail rises and falls in great gentle sighs, at least in com-
parison to the surrounding topography. This mead-
owed corridor through the mountains was so agreeable
to travel that old-time trappers—the Jim Bridgers and
Osborne Russells—called it the Thorofare.

We camped under the mountain called Hawks Rest, just outside the border of the park. I went off by myself, bathed in the Yellowstone, then took a short-cut back to camp. That was a mistake, because the ground was the consistency of Jell-O, and it swallowed my legs to midcalf. When I got back to camp, I was sweating profusely and pretty much entirely filthy—which required another trip, this one on a trail, back to the river for another bath.

So I was amazed early the next morning when I saw a huge bull moose *trotting* on his big pie-plate hooves through the same marsh that had nearly eaten me alive the day before. Low clouds scattered the newly risen sun in slanting pillars, an effect that is locally called God light. The moose, a deep auburn color in the God light, moved effortlessly through the mud and flowers, great muscles rolling in his immense shoulders. Beauty finds you where it will, and I was, at the time, squatting in the bushes performing my morning necessity.

We passed Hawks Rest, crossed the Yellowstone River on a wooden bridge, walked past Bridger Lake, and entered the park where a sign had fallen from a single ghost tree standing sentinel at the trail. It was a two-mile walk to the Thorofare Ranger Station, which meant we were halfway finished with the trip. Ironically, it was necessary (and, I suppose, polite) to contact the National Park Service, an agency of the U. S.

government, to secure permission to speak with the person living in the most remote cabin in the contiguous United States. The NPS would radio the ranger with the particulars of our arrival.

We saw in the distance a chinked log cabin, with a barn, a few outbuildings, and a treehouse, of the type kids and rangers enjoy. A sign on the door of the cabin said, THE RANGER ON DUTY HAS DEPARTED. So much for calling ahead.

No matter. We moved on around the three-lobed mountain called the Trident and found our assigned campsites in a thick forest of unburned lodgepole pine and Douglas fir. A small gray metal sign on the trail read, "6Z5," the number of the site we'd reserved. An arrow pointed the direction. (Yes, you have to make backcountry campsite reservations. The guidebooks listed in the "Bookshelf" section will tell you how to do it.)

Campsites are sometimes quite a distance from the trail—it had taken us twenty minutes to find this one. We crashed around in a glade of pungent, musky-smelling cow parsnip, a primeval-looking elephant-eared vegetation that rose up over our heads. Dave and Kara found the food pole: a long lodgepole log lashed to two growing pines, like a hitching post twelve feet high. The park provides the poles and expects backcountry visitors to toss a rope over and pull their food up out of bears' reach. This isn't just a bureaucratic annoyance. Bears have olfactory systems far superior to those of bloodhounds. They can smell, say, salami from miles away.

So it's best to hang your food. Some wise campers even hang the clothes they wear while cooking. All wise campers hang their pots and dishes, clean or not. They camp upwind of the food stash and several hundred yards away.

So we hung our food, then crashed through the cow parsnip jungle, which gave way to a vast expanse of meadow. That is where we set up our tents: on the very edge of the Thorofare, the Mother of all Meadows.

I could see for fifteen miles in one direction, at a guess, ten in another. A fierce wind arose, and the grasses and the sedges and the forbs and the flowers danced a brief mad fandango, then all at once everything went calm and dusk settled over the land. The moon rose, Mars scowled down, the Milky Way spread across the known universe, and nowhere, in any direction I looked, was there a single light.

I was still thinking about the privilege of solitude the next morning. In six days we'd seen two hikers and two horse-packing parties, all back in the Bridger-Teton. We'd seen nobody in the Thorofare.

Suddenly a sound like gunfire echoed off the walls of the mountains on either side of the rocky corridor that enfolded the meadow. It was a bright, windy day, and we'd been hearing these thunderclaps reverberating all about us every few hours. Tom said they were ghost trees falling in the distance, and indeed, this time we could see it. Across a narrow part of the meadow, in a fringing ghost forest on the flank of the mountain opposite, a huge lodgepole had toppled, caught on a neighboring tree for a moment, then fallen to earth in a series of tremendous crashing echoes.

The ghost forests date mostly from what the Park Service is pleased to call "the fire event of 1988." New timber is growing in the midst of the ghost forests, living lodgepoles now eight and ten feet high and growing at the rate of about ten inches a year. Soon, as the older trees crash around them, the new growth will accelerate, each tree growing straight and fast, racing the others to the sun. In ten more years, the forest will be 16 to 20 feet high, and a hundred years from now the trees will be 110 or 130 feet high, and there will be another fire event. People are more than willing to argue this point—fire can be stopped, or it shouldn't be stopped, or it ought to be purposely set—but this is my reading of the history and natural history of the land. I believe we are privileged to see the forest regenerate itself in our lifetimes. We're at that point in the cycle: about a dozen years into a turn-around of a century or more.

We camped under Colter Peak and high-stepped across the marshy meadow of the Thorofare to the Yellowstone River. Evidence on the muddy banks showed that this immense meadow was a thoroughfare for life in general, with no particular nod to the human variety. All the tracks were fresh, but one tended to notice the grizzly first. You can place a stick across the front paw print of a grizzly, and all the nails of the paw will be on one side. You can't do this with the print of a black bear. So we knew this guy was a griz. His front foot was twelve inches across, by actual measurement.

Nearby we saw a cylinder of scat with a little bit of hair in it. The wolf tracks leading away were bigger than those of the coyote that seemed to have come by later. A raven had strutted about the bank, and the beaver's track was plain enough as well: an endearing pigeon-toed gait, with the flat rake of the tail dragging behind.

The next morning we woke to the deep, aching, eerie howling of wolves in the near distance. It is a sound that sends a shimmer of gooseflesh down the arms and up the back.

Tom had a special mission that day. He was going to take us to see a waterfall he'd found a while ago, one that wasn't in the *Waterfalls* book. The authors of that controversial work admitted that "we would be fools to believe we had found every waterfall in Yellowstone." Once again they were right, and we had proof of that only ten or twelve miles out of our way. Tom, who is one of those people who would rather not clutter up wilderness maps with a lot of names, told me, "You can't give the location" when I wrote about it.

"What about all the people who live in the city and have mental problems?" I argued. "Giving the location and naming the falls might *help* them."

"If you do that," Tom explained sadly, "I'll have to kill you." He didn't care about city dwellers' sanity, not even a little bit.

It was, let us say, a goodly walk, and it took us up to the top of a low plateau, where the fire event of 1988 had been particularly fierce. The ghost forest stretched on forever, on all sides, as far as the eye could see. A brutal wind shrieked through the bones of the forest, and we could hear the trees creaking, creaking, creaking with their craving to finally and irrevocably fall.

Coming through the forest, moving toward us along the trail, was a man on horseback who turned out to be backcountry ranger Bob Jackson. He had a bunch of work to do and not much time to chat. He lived in the Thorofare cabin, he said, from June 1 to the end of October, and had since 1978. Used to be, he caught a lot of poachers coming into the park during hunting season looking for prize animals: elk and mountain sheep, mostly. There is less poaching going on today, but bad guys are still out there. Bob had seen their tracks and planned to get them. "You know," he said, "almost every poacher, when I finally caught him, he cried." Bob Jackson liked that: catching crybaby poachers.

He asked us where we were going, and Tom described the waterfall. "One of the prettiest ones in the park," Bob said.

"You mean," I asked, "you know about this fall? Why don't you name it and take credit for its discovery?" Bob Jackson looked at me in the manner I imagine he looks at poachers. I didn't immediately burst into tears, though on sober reflection I believe that would have been the proper response. "It was a *joke,* Bob," I wanted to call after him as he rode off through the ghost forest.

Hours later we reached the shores of Yellowstone Lake, which stretched out blue-gray as far as the eye could see, 14 miles wide, 20 miles long, with an average depth of 140 feet. It is one of the largest mountain lakes on earth, the largest in the United States over 7,000 feet (it is situated at 7,733 feet). It has 110 miles of shoreline, so I can tell you that the unnamed waterfall was about half a mile from the lake—that doesn't narrow it down too much.

Tom found it one day when he was "dinking around," looking for a spring actually, because Tom will fill his canteen from a spring in preference to pumping and purifying water. He'd seen a lush hillside, covered over in cow parsnip and mossy rock— good signs of water—and about 150 feet above, he found water gushing out of the side of the hill. It fell 18 or 20 feet and then cascaded down some rocks for another 35 to 40 feet. I thought it was all the more appealing because it was a waterfall that started as a spring. It flowed out of the ground, out into space, then dropped against the rock wall. We filled our canteens, drank greedily, and sat suffering ice cream headaches for ten minutes or so. The water was 44 degrees according to my temperature-sensing watch.

Now, since we'd gone twelve miles out of our way and were moving at something less than three miles an hour, we were going to be late getting into camp. It is not usually a good idea to walk at night in the park. It's not even a good idea to walk at twilight because, as Tom explained, bears are "crepuscular," which means that they tend to feed in the half-light of dawn and dusk. I was thinking about that as we crossed a creek, and there, on the trail, was the track of a large grizzly. It was new: I could see the ridges like fingerprints on the pads of its toes. "About two minutes ahead of us," Tom said.

"You think so?" How does a person *know* something like that? Is it long experience? Exhaustive study? Turns out it's a matter of simple observation, and I felt foolish as soon as Tom showed me what he'd seen.

"Look here," he said. There, beside the track, were several drops of water in the dusty soil, and they were moving forward along with the tracks, so that it looked as if someone had been walking along carrying a wet rug, except that this was a grizzly track and the wet rug was the wet bear skin attached to the wet grizzly. We'd just crossed a creek, and so had the bear. The water drops were drying up even as I looked at them. The griz *was* about two minutes ahead of us. Apparently we'd scared him up out of his daybed, and he was fleeing before us.

We were moving through some creekside willows twelve feet high. I didn't much care for this visually limited and claustrophobic world, so I sang to alert the animal to my presence. My singing has had the effect of clearing human habitations of all life. Maybe it would work with bears.

"'Hang on, Sloopy,'" I sang, and so on. After several minutes Tom said, "Maybe the bear will come and put you out of your misery."

But I had my bear-repellent pepper spray out and was ready. "Tom," I said, full of false bravado, "that guy wants to get crepuscular on me, I'm going to show him a whole new world of crepuscularity."

Presently the sun set, and we were walking in the dark, with headlamps, along the north side of the southeast arm of Yellowstone Lake, until we found our reserved campsite at about eleven-thirty at night. The sky was perfectly clear, the moon almost full, and waves lapped gently on the beach, so that it looked as if a palm tree ought to be silhouetted against the sky. But on this last day of July the temperature stood somewhere to the south of twenty degrees. It was damn cold.

I left that morning, as planned. Tom stayed for another week.

The Goblin Labyrinth

THREE WEEKS LATER TOM AND I TOOK OUR SECOND trip into the backcountry. Just the two of us made our way through sagebrush-littered flats of the Lamar Valley, at the northeast end of the park, moving due south, toward Hoodoo Peak and Hoodoo Basin, an area that P. W. Norris, who had been appointed park superintendent in 1877, called "the Goblin Labyrinth."

Tom and I were taking big loops around bison that weighed in the neighborhood of one ton. "Two days after you left the lake I saw something that I thought only existed in folklore," he told me. "An evening rain squall passed across the lake, and the last of the rain hung in the air. There was a light then, and I turned to see the full moon, which was just rising, on the horizon. When I turned back and looked into what was left of the rain, I thought I could see a faint silvery sort of line, and then it grew bigger and bent around until I was looking at a kind of rainbow in negative. A moonbow."

"Any colors?" I asked, envious.

"It was all bluish white." The way Tom described it, the color was like something made of electricity.

The bison we were skirting regarded us with bovine indifference. I'd missed the vaporous display by forty-eight hours. Experience of a lifetime going on up at Yellowstone Lake, and I was down in town having a drink at the Owl.

As if to put a certain emphasis on my regret, it began to rain intermittently. Tom, as it turned out, didn't carry rain gear. If he had to, he walked wet; if it was a cold rain, he walked fast.

"B-but," I stammered, "you're a guide. You work search and rescue."

"I'm not saying it's right," Tom said. "When you grow up on a cattle ranch in South Dakota, you just don't have a lot of experience with rain." He thought a bit. "Rain was good."

The trail took us along Miller Creek, over an undulating land of creeks flowing down into a narrow valley. Meadows were few. Ghost forests dominated. It wasn't very scenic at all: twenty miles and more of nothing much to see. At one point Tom took me off the trail, and there in the high grass, with standing dead all about, were a few burned logs from an old cabin and a pile of stones that had been the chimney. Scattered about were some rusted Dutch ovens, a cast-iron frying pan, and an enamel pan. Tom had found the place some years ago, when he'd stepped off the trail to do the necessary thing. He'd shown it to park personnel.

"See this glass?" Tom said. He was holding up a thick shard, of a vaguely purple hue. "That color is manganese," he said. "It came from Germany. During the First World War, America stopped importing German products, and later glass products are clear. So judging by the glass, this cabin was built sometime before 1917." The rusted nails on the ground told another story. "They're round," Tom explained. "Round wire nails came in about 1900. Before that, people used square nails." So that dated the cabin pretty closely between 1900 and 1917. It was, most likely, a poacher's cabin.

Two days and twenty miles in, we arrived at the Upper Miller Creek Patrol Station and ran into the Lamar backcountry supervising ranger, Mike Ross. He was tall and blond and handsome and is one of the few men I've ever met who doesn't look like a complete dork in a ranger uniform.

Mike is one of the Park Service personnel who

doesn't agree with the concept of the *Waterfalls* book. "I grew up in the park," he said. "I know it pretty well, and those guys did some real exploration. But I had problems with the naming. I wrote [*Waterfalls* author] Lee Whittlesey an e-mail and told him that the thrill he got naming and locating these falls was one he stole from every subsequent visitor." We stayed the night near the cabin and chatted with Mike until long after dark. "I don't get a lot of company here," he said. "And the people I do see usually turn back at this point."

"Why?" I asked. The Hoodoo Basin, with its weird formations, was just over the hill, about eight miles away and 2,000 feet above.

"Well, sometimes they've overestimated what they can do," Mike said. "And then it's a long boring walk. I mean, there aren't a lot of sweeping views, and it's mostly burned. And finally, they don't want to make the two-thousand-foot climb." He pointed to the forested wall behind the cabin. "We call that Parachute Mountain," he said.

"How many people actually get to the Hoodoo Basin?" I asked.

Mike pulled out some kind of Palm Pilot, scratched on it with a stylus, and said, "I downloaded this at the backcountry office a few days ago. As of August twentieth, there were three permits for the year. You guys are one. I doubt if twenty-five sets of eyes see the Hoodoos in any given year."

Parachute Mountain is a bastard, there's no doubt about it, a cruel set of switchbacks that took us two long hours of trudging. We topped out on a grassy hillside of long sloping meadows that gave way to cool unburned forest at 9,500 feet. All about, lying on the ground near the trail, were obsidian chips: arrowheads and spear points and scrapers. These were tools chipped out of rock with rock by men who had found a pleasant and militarily advantageous place to work. Ahead, we could see the summit of Parker Peak and the saddle on its shoulder where park superintendent P. W. Norris saw the remains of a few dozen wiki-ups in 1880.

We walked up to the saddle, which was a grassy expanse, and several dozen elk fled before us. Quite a few old sticks were lying about, but no timber was near. Indians did not always carry heavy buffalo-skin teepees. Especially when they were raiding or hunting, they traveled light and often sheltered in hastily built wiki-ups, which are conical timber lodges made of sticks eight to ten feet long and about as big around as a man's arm. It was pretty to think that the weathered sticks we saw on the ground were the remains of the wiki-ups Norris reported on almost 125 years ago. He didn't say who might have built them—Crow or

Bannock or Shoshone—but these were the last truly free Indians to inhabit the park. By 1878 all the tribes had been defeated in war or were imprisoned on reservations. Perhaps the Nez Perce, on their last desperate run, led by the brilliant Chief Joseph, had built the wiki-ups. (But Norris had reported the remains of forty structures, which may have housed a hundred people; Chief Joseph was traveling with about two hundred warriors and about five hundred women and children.)

Tom and I walked up to the summit of Parker Peak, 10,203 feet high according to the map, and I could see the high peaks that fringed the park. A bald eagle cut spiraling circles in the sky—we were looking down on him. In the far distance, plumes of smoke from the fires of summer mushroomed up into the cobalt sky: a forest was burning down south toward Jackson Hole, and another big one up north at Fridley Creek, near the Montana town where Tom and I live.

Tom strolled down a short ridge running south off the summit. Where it dead-ended in cliffs, someone had built a small enclosure of rocks set on edge and fit together with other smaller rocks wedged into the interstices of the construction. The whole affair was about six by nine feet, an oval enclosure protected from the wind and overlooking the Lamar River to the southwest and the Beartooth Plateau to the northeast. It was a place where men came to discover what was sacred. A vision quest site, and not on any map I know of.

We came down Parker Peak on the north side, skirting a permanent snowfield: an oval perhaps 125 feet high and 50 feet across. It was set in a declivity of talus and, when we first saw it, glittered like a mirror under the noon sun. Later in the day we could see that the snow was uniformly soiled, streaked with rock- and dirtfall from above.

We came back to the saddle and made for the Hoodoo Basin, our destination. Superintendent Norris, in his 1880 report, had noted that some prospectors, working the head of the Upper Lamar River in 1870, had stumbled on "a region of countless remnants of erosion, so wild, weird and spectral that they named it the 'Hoodoo' or 'Goblin Land.'" Norris himself preferred the name "Goblin Labyrinth."

The trail led to a basin under the rounded grassy summit of Hoodoo Peak. It appeared that 500 feet of vertical slope had eroded away from the mountain, leaving a haphazard labyrinth of oddly shaped reddish-gray columns. There was one pillar, 100 feet high at a guess, upon which a large rock was balanced, precariously. It looked like nothing so much as a small car resting on its front bumper with its back wheels in the air. The formation was very much like one P. W. Norris had sketched in 1880. Could that top rock have held its position for more than 120 years? It occurred to me that I had arrived at an unfamiliar intersection between geology and acrobatics.

I moved below the permanently precarious hard-rock circus and walked around a high flat blade of standing stone. It was growing late, and the sky above was still blue, but in the basin, where we were, shadows fell all about. I looked up at the flat rock rising 60 or 70 feet above me, and it resolved itself into a face, with a central protrusion of nose, and a large pyramidal hat above, of the sort that might be worn by a shaman or priest of some alien religion. But what made me stumble backward, startled in the silence, was the perfectly animate pair of eyes staring down at me. They were a cool, luminescent living blue. I believe I said something clever, like, "Whoa," as I wheeled backward, then stood still, pinned motionless under the intense blue gaze of the rock. I lived through five very odd seconds until the eyes resolved themselves into two round holes in the flattish rock. The basin was all in shadow, but I was looking up through the holes directly into the blue of the western sky.

Tom and I spent two days alone in the Goblin Labyrinth. The nights were deliciously creepy. The moon, half full behind us, illuminated the various figures in a pale light broken by irregular shadows. The stars, cold and bright, glittered through holes in the rock. They wheeled overhead as we sat for hours watching the shadows shift so that the rock figures assumed alternate shapes: a horse's head, a fierce crouching lion, a failed saguaro cactus, a sorcerer's apprentice.

The next day we climbed Hoodoo Peak, which at 10,546 feet was 1,000 feet above the basin. There were more goblins set higher on the mountain, and they were less eroded than the ones in the basin, so that from a distance they looked rather like the heads on Easter Island, only bunched closely together, as if conspiring in the wind. There were some fanciful columns and balancing acts. I rather liked the one that looked like a pig on a stilt.

Still, it was the basin that drew me back at dusk the next night. I went around the front side of the flat rock and stood in its shadow in order to stare it directly in the eyes. And the damn thing *winked* at me. "Whoa," I said.

"What?" Tom asked.

"The rock is winking at me."

I climbed up on a scree slope to get a better view. Aha! Some small bird, probably an owl, was moving in and out of the eye, perching there for some moments as it scanned the ground for rodents. The owl had blocked the sky and caused the rock face to wink.

I dragged Tom to that vantage point and told him

that an owl was making the rock wink. By that time—
naturally—the bird had flown the coop, so to speak.
Tom glanced up into the empty eye socket, then
stared at me for an uncomfortable moment.

"Have you been smoking something?" he asked.

The River of Reliable Rainbows

A T THE FAR SOUTHWEST CORNER OF THE PARK is an area called the Bechler, named for the main river course. If the Bechler ever ran a personal ad seeking companionship, it would be a pretty sappy one: "If you like hot tubs and rainbows and waterfalls, you'll like me. I'm the Bechler."

This time our group consisted of Tom and me, Dave Long, and our emergency room crew from the first trip—Eileen Ralicke and Kara Kreitlow—and Liz Schultz, a friend and a local interior decorator who was in charge of camp decor. We drove to Ashton, Idaho, then down the gravel road that led to the Bechler entrance. "We're doing this," I reminded everyone, "in the name of city dwellers' sanity." Just in case anyone thought we were simply out having fun.

And maybe it wouldn't be all that enjoyable. We were certainly pushing the weather. It was late September, and though it can snow on you any month of the year in Yellowstone, September and October are famous for days of mild summer temperatures, followed by heavy wet snows accumulating sometimes several feet in a matter of twenty-four hours. Often roads are closed due to heavy snowfall—in August. And in 2001 it snowed pretty hard in June. A hiker in sandals, who would have lost his feet to frostbite, had to be rescued by helicopter.

"It won't snow on us," I told my hiking companions, "because I lead a good and virtuous life."

"We're dead," Dave Long said.

The trail was essentially flat and took us through the autumnal grasses of the immense Bechler Meadows. The flowers of summer had vanished, and mountain blue birds were massing in groups of four and five and six, deciding precisely when to start their trip south.

We camped at a site in the meadow. It was the season of rut for elk, and we could hear various males bugling in the distance. This high-pitched noise is almost like the shriek air makes escaping from a balloon when the breath tube is stretched flat. It moderates down in tone to a kind of pained whine, as if the animal were saying, "Mate with me, mate with me, all of you, mate with me." The bugling echoes for miles across the meadow.

Elk were mating now—the males were fighting,

and they had to chase the females, which depleted the fat that both sexes had accumulated over the summer and thereby diminished their chances of surviving the winter. "It would be better for the elk," Dave said as we prepared dinner, "if the females just gave it up."

All three women stared at him. A silence ensued. Dave said, "Or I could be wrong."

Coyotes yipped and howled, harmonizing with the elk, and their vocalizations sounded nothing at all like the deep eerie sounds made by wolves.

In the morning the grasses were frosted over, glittering in the sun, and we could see the snow-covered ridge of the Tetons in the southern distance. A bull moose was trotting alongside of the meadow, near a fringe of trees. Moving out ahead, a female was running rapidly away and not about to just give it up at all. The male animal was making a series of revolting sounds: it started with a kind of *eh-eh-eh,* followed by a tormented swallowing, and then a repulsive noise like someone seriously vomiting ("Mate with me! Oh God, I'm sick. Mate with me!").

Tom took his camera out and trotted along parallel to the moose, about 300 yards away. The big animal glanced over and dipped his big rack of horns from one side to the other like a man shaking his finger no. Tom retreated strategically, took refuge behind some trees, then crouched low behind a line of bushes, trying to get a shot of the lovesick moose in the Bechler Meadows dawn. I sat in my camp chair, drinking coffee and watching the moose races.

The weather held—it's my good and virtuous life—and it was actually hot at noon. While Dave fished, the rest of us swam in the river, which is fed above by numerous hot springs and not nearly as cold as one might expect. Nor, I must confess, is it precisely warm.

Refreshed, we began moving up Bechler Canyon, which is famous for its waterfalls. The topography is this: centrally located in the Bechler region is the Pitchstone Plateau, which is nearly 9,000 feet high. It drops off to the southwest, and water flows down a rocky sloping area that terminates in any number of sheer cliffs. This is Cascade Corner. The waterfalls of Cascade Corner drop off into the Bechler Meadows or the Falls River Basin.

Ouzel Falls is west of the main trail, dropping off a rock ridge at the entrance to the Bechler River canyon. From our first vantage point, we had no sense of water moving. The fall looked like a distant mirror glittering in the sun. There seemed to be no trail to the fall—none we could find—and we bushwhacked over animal trails and down timber, then moved up a deeply wooded canyon and stood at the foot of the fall, which drops 230 feet and is one of Yellowstone's tallest. It was now three in the afternoon, and the sun had cleared the trees on both sides of the narrow canyon. Rainbows danced in the spray at the base of Ouzel Falls.

Eileen scrambled up some talus to shower in the shifting shards of color. To see a rainbow, you need a light source behind you and water vapor floating on air in front. I moved this way and that, in order to position the sun and spray to enhance the colors floating and shifting at the base of the fall. The map suggested that a great many of the falls on and around the Bechler region faced generally south, which meant the sun would shine directly on them at least part of the day. And that meant that every day in which there was sun, there'd be a rainbow or two or three as well. You could count on them: I thought of the Bechler as the River of Reliable Rainbows.

Over the next several days we moved up the Bechler and courageously endured the sight of many waterfalls generating many rainbows. Colonnade Falls, for instance, just off the trail, is a two-step affair, with a 35-foot plunge above, a pool, and a 67-foot fall below. The lower fall was enfolded in curving basalt wall. The gray rock had formed itself into consecutive columns more in the Doric tradition than the Corinthian. It had a certain wild nobility, Yellowstone's own Parthenon, with falls and a fountain.

Iris Falls, a short distance above Colonnade, tumbles

45 feet into a churning green pool. Above, and parallel to the trail, the river becomes a chute of white water roaring over steep slabs of smooth rock.

Some hours later the canyon widened, and the trail moved through a meadow where vaguely oval hot pools 10 and 20 and 30 feet across steamed in the sun. In some of the pools there were bits and shards of what appeared to be rusted sheet metal, as if someone had driven a Model T into the water eighty years ago. In fact, the shards were living colonies of microbes.

"If you cut into them," Dave Long, the biochemist, said, "you see that the top layer uses the longest visible light, the second layer uses shorter light, and so on, until all the light is used." I stared at the cooperative colony, and it still looked like chunks of old cars to me.

We branched off the main trail and followed the Ferris Fork of the Bechler. This little-used path drops down into another narrow meadow, where there are a number of hot springs and pools. Steam rises off the boiling creeks in strange curvilinear patterns. A spectacular terrace of precipitated material stood on the opposite bank of the river, a kind of Mammoth Hot Springs in miniature. Hot water from the pool above ran down the bank of the terrace, which was striated in several colors: wet brown and garish pumpkin and overachieving moss, all interspersed with running channels of steaming water and lined in creamy beige.

The north side of the terrace was a Day-Glo green, overlaid with a precipitate of flawless cream. Just at river level the green rock formed a pool perhaps ten feet in diameter, and the surface of this pool was the color of cream as well.

Features like this exist almost nowhere else on earth and are the reason that there is a Yellowstone Park today.

Steam poured from the top of the terrace, which consisted of two hot pools fitting together like an hourglass. In the front pool, a constant eruption of bubbles from below made a sound like a jet in the near distance.

We followed the Ferris Fork up the drainage that led to the Pitchstone Plateau, passing five waterfalls in the space of a couple hours' walk. The top fall was unnamed—another one not in the *Waterfalls* book— but the bottom four were all on the map: Wahhi, Sluice- way, Gwinna, and Tendoy. All were shadowed in foliage and faced vaguely north, so they were not good rain- bow falls. Tom thought they were all awfully pretty. I kept my own counsel. I like rainbows.

We came back down to the meadow near the steaming terrace and sat in the river, just where one of the bigger hot streams poured into the cold water of the Ferris Fork. It is illegal—not to say suicidal—to bathe in any of the thermal features of the park. But when these features empty into the river, at what is called a hot pot, swimming and soaking are perfectly acceptable. So we were soaking off our long walk, talking about our favorite waterfalls, and discussing rainbows when it occurred to us that the moon was full. There wasn't a hint of foul weather. And if you had a clear sky and a waterfall facing in just the right direction . . .

Over the course of a couple of days we hiked back down the canyon to the Boundary Creek Trail and followed it to Dunanda Falls, which is only about eight miles from the ranger station at the entrance to the park. Dunanda is a 150-foot-high plunge facing generally south, so that in the afternoons reliable rainbows dance over the rocks at its base. It is the archetype of all western waterfalls. *Dunanda* is an Indian name, in Shoshone it means "straight down," which is a pretty good description of the plunge.

I make this exception: water rolls over the lip at the top, then catches in a series of notched pools just below; these pools empty themselves intermittently. Eileen, always one to test the shower, said that it felt like one of those pulsing showerheads, except that the alternation was between a gentle spray and a ten-gallon bucketload.

We had to walk three miles back toward the ranger station and our assigned campsite. We planned to set up our tents, eat, hang our food, and walk back to Dunanda Falls in the dark, using headlamps. We could be there by ten or eleven. At that time the full moon would clear the east ridge of the downriver canyon and would be shining directly on the fall.

Walking at night is never a happy proposition, and this particular evening stroll involved five stream crossings, mostly on old logs, and took a lot longer than we'd anticipated. Still, we beat the moon to the fall.

Most of us took up residence in one or another of the hot pots. Presently the moon, like a floodlight, rose over the canyon rim. The falling water took on a silver tinge, and the rock wall, which had looked gold under the sun, was now a slick black so the contrast of water and rock was incomparably stark. The pools below the lip of the fall were glowing, as from within, with a pale blue light. And then it started at the base of the fall: just a diagonal line in the spray that ran from the lower east to the upper west side of the wall.

"It's going to happen," I told Kara, who was sitting beside me in one of the hot pots.

Where falling water hit the rock at the base of the fall and exploded upward in vapor, the light was very bright. It concentrated itself in a shining ball. The diagonal line was above and slowly began to bend until, in the fullness of time (ten minutes, maybe), it formed a perfectly symmetrical bow, shining silver blue under the moon. The color was vaguely electrical.

Kara said she could see colors in the moonbow, and when I looked very hard, I thought I could make out a faint line of reddish orange above, and some deep violet at the bottom. Both colors were very pale, flickering, like bad fluorescent light.

In any case, it was exhilarating, the experience of a lifetime: an entirely perfect moonbow, silver and iridescent, all shining and spectral there at the base of Dunanda Falls. The hot pot itself was a luxury, and I considered myself a pretty swell fellow, doing all this for the sanity of city dwellers, who need such things more than anyone else. I even thought of naming the moonbow: Cahill's Luminescence. Something like that. Otherwise, someone else might take credit for it.

A SELECTED YELLOWSTONE BOOKSHELF,

being, in fact, a bunch of books that I own and use frequently, plus a few volumes that will be of special interest to the first-time visitor, such as . . .

The Very Best Practical Guide to Yellowstone

*Lonely Planet Yellowstone and Grand Teton
National Parks,*
Bradley Mayhew, Andrew Dean Nystrom, and Amy
Marr, Lonely Planet, 2003.

The introduction is by Tim Cahill, which shouldn't
prejudice you against this book—it is simply the best
practical guide to the park. If you buy only one book
to prepare for your Yellowstone trip, this is the one. It
has stuff about where to stay, where to eat, which hiking trails to take, and how much everything costs, as
well as explanations of the various attractions and
necessary information about the history, geology, and
topography of the park, not to mention a number of
suggested itineraries for visits of one or two days or
weeks.

DAY HIKING GUIDES

A Ranger's Guide to Yellowstone Day Hikes,
Roger Anderson and Carol Shively Anderson,
Montana Magazine, 2000.

This is my favorite book of day hikes. The authors, husband and wife rangers, don't just tell you where to go, they help you understand what you are seeing. It's like going on a ranger hike without the irritating crowd and the guy who interrupts your stupid question with his own brainless interrogatory.

Best Easy Day Hikes Yellowstone,
Bill Schneider, Falcon Publishing, 1997.

These are indeed easy, but Schneider—who's written the best comprehensive backcountry hiking guide—knows some tricky shortcuts on the longer trails.

Day Hiking Yellowstone,
Tom Carter, Day Hiking Press, 1998.

This extraordinarily useful little book is cheap ($4.95) and small enough to fit in a pocket. A hike selector allows you to select waterfalls, geysers, wildflowers, wildlife, and much else. It is divided into short hikes, as well as half-day and full-day treks.

Day Hikes in Yellowstone National Park,
Robert Stone, Day Hike Books, 2000.

This book offers straightforward but not particularly inspired descriptions of fifty-four day hikes, a lot more hikes than the other books give you.

BACKCOUNTRY HIKING GUIDES

Hiking Yellowstone National Park,
Bill Schneider, Falcon Publishing, 1997.

This comprehensive guide offers short hikes as well as ten-day overnighters. It is well-organized and full of necessary advice on planning, "getting there," and obtaining backcountry permits. The various campsites are rated. The maps, however, are generally schematics; the author advises you to buy topos or *Trails Illustrated* maps (and tells you where to get them).

Yellowstone Trails: A Hiking Guide,
Mark C. Marschall, Yellowstone Association, 1999.

Spiral-bound, this book has good maps, sufficient for planning hikes and navigating as long as you stay on maintained trails. Mileages are noted. Also included is invaluable information about dealing with bears, purifying water, and getting that backcountry camp-site you want.

A GOOD SHORT GUIDE

Yellowstone: The Official Guide to Touring America's First National Park,
no author named, Yellowstone Association, 1998.

I suspect a committee wrote this book, but it was a committee that, surprisingly, communicates in plain and effective English. There's not much information on hotels, campsites, or how to obtain backcountry sites, but it's perfect for car campers doing day hikes. The book is the size of a large magazine and not something you might carry on a trek, but it has a pic-torial field guide to the plants and animals you are most likely to see from the road.

ONE GUIDE THAT PRESENTS ME WITH CERTAIN PHILOSOPHICAL PROBLEMS

The Guide to Yellowstone Waterfalls and Their Discovery,
Paul Rubinstein, Lee H. Whittlesey, and Mike Stevens, Westcliffe Publishers, 2000.

I discuss my problems with this book in the text. Is it on my bookshelf? Yep.

BOOKS THAT PRESENT A GOOD OVERVIEW OF YELLOWSTONE PARK

Yellowstone: A Visitor's Companion,
George Wuerthner, Stackpole Books, 1992.

This book is neatly divided into sections, so you can review the geology or history of the park easily. It has sections on weather, flora, and fauna as well as information about fires and ecological challenges to the Greater Yellowstone Ecosystem.

Yellowstone: Official National Park Handbook,
U.S Department of the Interior, 2001.

I know, I know, it's from the U.S. government, so I figured it wouldn't be any good either, but this brief book was authored by award-winning nature writer David Rains Wallace and is informative as well as poetic.

History

The Yellowstone Story, 2 vols.,
Aubrey L. Haines, Yellowstone Library and Museum
Association in cooperation with Colorado
Associated University Press, 1977.

Unsurpassed. Indispensable.

Journal of a Trapper,
Osborne Russell, Bison Books, 1965.

According to historian Aubrey Haines, this is "perhaps the best account of the life of a fur trapper in the
Rocky Mountains when the trade was at its peak."
That was between 1834 and 1843. A keen observer,
Russell was also an engaging writer. In a preface he
warned, "Reader, if you are in search of travels of a
Classical and Scientific tourist, please to lay this Vol-
ume down, and pass on, for this simply informs you
what a trapper has seen." The descriptions are so
accurate that you can see the land he described today.

The Discovery of Yellowstone Park,
Nathaniel Pitt Langford, written in 1905; Bison
Books, 1972.

Langford's fascinating and somewhat self-congratulatory
account of the 1870 Washburn Expedition. As histo-

rian Aubrey Haines points out in his introduction to the 1972 edition, the title is erroneous: Langford "recorded definitive exploration, not discovery." I have problems with the sort of gratuitous chest-thumping that confuses documentation with discovery.

GEOLOGY

Interpreting the Landscape: Recent and Ongoing Geology of Grand Teton and Yellowstone National Parks,
John M. Good and Kenneth L. Pierce, Grand Teton Natural History Association in cooperation with the National Park Service, 2002.

Fire and ice and earth-shattering eruptions—this short book, written for laypeople, helped me get some kind of grasp on all the geology going on in and around Yellowstone, and that's saying a lot. I'm a guy with geological dyslexia.

Windows into the Earth,
Robert B. Smith and Lee J. Siegel, Oxford University Press, 2000.

This is the definitive treatment, or so I've been told by geologists who should know. I spent a splendid afternoon in the Norris Geyser Basin with author Smith, but I haven't yet read the book. This is why I have geological dyslexia. I'm ashamed of myself.

Biology

The Wolves of Yellowstone,
Michael K. Phillips and Douglas W. Smith, Voyageur
Press, 1996.

This oral and written history of wolf reintroduction,
by the two project leaders and others of note, is as
clear a picture as you will get about why the wolf was
reintroduced to the park, and how. It's not so good if
you hate wolves. Me? I got goose bumps.

Life at High Temperatures,
Thomas D. Brock, Yellowstone Association, 1994.

The husband-and-wife team Thomas and Louise Brock
discovered that the earthy-colored scum on Yellowstone's thermal ponds contains microbes, thermophiles,
creatures living in acidic waters that until then—1965—
were considered too hot to support life. Here Dr. Brock
gives us a break and writes a highly simplified explana-
tion of life at high temperatures.

Scats and Tracks of the Rocky Mountains,
James C. Halfpenny, Globe Pequot Press, 2001.

This is a must-have. Is that the track of a black bear or
a grizzly? (It is really easy to tell, by the way.) Who left

that pile on the trail—a coyote or a wolf? Halfpenny provides a field guide to seventy wildlife species in a book that fits in your back pocket. Don't leave camp without it. Illustrated by Todd Telander.

Safe Travel in Bear Country,
Gary Brown, Lyons and Burford, 1996.

You know you have to hang your food if you're overnighting in the backcountry. But how do you do it? How much rope do you need? What is "bear sign"? Which bear is most dangerous? If a bear charges, do you run or play dead? Should you carry bear spray? All these questions are answered and more—you need this book.

Two Books on Yellowstone Place Names

Yellowstone Place Names: Mirrors of History,
Aubrey L. Haines, University Press of Colorado, 1996.

The retired park historian organizes his book rather conceptually, introducing each chapter with a review of the historical period: names drawn from Native American life in the park, for instance, or from the fur trade. It's good reading, but tough to use as a reference.

Yellowstone Place Names,
Lee H. Whittlesey, Montana Historical Society
Press, 1988.

The present park historian organizes his book alphabetically. I find myself reaching for this one more often than Haines's, mostly because it is easier to use as a reference.

Read It or Die

Death in Yellowstone,
Lee H. Whittlesey, Court Wayne Press, 1995.

One reviewer called this book "morbidly fascinating," and it is, but the author's central message, shouted out in capital letters, is "PLAY SAFELY." Not a bad idea. More than three hundred deaths are recounted here. If a body of water is bubbling, there's a good chance it's boiling, so a person would die horribly if he decided to jump in, for instance, to save a dog. Bison gore people every year in Yellowstone, and that one over there weighs two thousand pounds and can run three times faster than an Olympic sprinter. Please don't try to put your four-year-old daughter on its back. The cute picture isn't worth her life, or even yours. Yes, all the animals here are real, and they're all wild. The water in Yellowstone Lake averages 41 degrees in the middle of the summer. You'd last twenty minutes in water that temperature: so how far from shore do you want to paddle that canoe? *Death* should probably be required reading for anyone who wants to enter the park.

Maps

Trails Illustrated
P.O. Box 4357
Evergreeen, CO 80437–4357
(800) 962–1643

These maps are sufficient for most users—that is, people who stay on the trails. There is a map of the park as a whole and four separate maps of Yellowstone in quadrants.

USGS 7.5 Minute Quadrangles (commonly called topos) are available from many local outdoor stores or can be ordered directly from:

Map Distribution
U.S. Geological Survey
Box 25286 Federal Center
Denver, CO 80225

Acknowledgments

I AM A WRITER AND QUICK TO NOTE UNATTRIB-
uted citations of my work. For that reason I've tried,
in the text, to credit every quote I've swiped from
another writer. Sometimes, inadvertently, a citation
slips by. In general, if something I've said makes me
look brilliant in the field of geology or biology or sci-
ence in particular, I probably took it from a book
listed in "A Selected Yellowstone Bookshelf."

Perceptive readers of my work will see echoes of
stories I wrote long ago for *Outside* magazine, among
others. The long section on backcountry travel in this
book appeared, in a shorter and somewhat different
form, in *National Geographic Adventure* magazine. The
story won the National Magazine Award, which I
shared with writer Jack Gorman, who did what is
called the service aspects of that piece. You have seen
that I am not very interested in service—in telling you

how to get there, where to stay, and how much things cost. This is a failing I hope I've remedied by listing several books in the back of this one that are entirely devoted to such things.

I am more interested in suggesting ways to think about the park and its significance. I'm especially interested in the exhilaration anyone with a heart feels while walking Yellowstone Park.

ABOUT THE AUTHOR

TIM CAHILL IS THE AUTHOR OF SEVEN PREVIOUS books, including *Hold the Enlightenment, A Wolverine Is Eating My Leg, Jaguars Ripped My Flesh,* and *Pass the Butterworms.* He is an editor-at-large for *Outside* magazine, and his work appears in *National Geographic Adventure, The New York Times Book Review,* and other national publications. He lives in Montana.